Conscious Creation 101

Michael Lightweaver
lightweave@aol.com

Mountain Light Publishing
PO Box 18909
Asheville, NC. 28814, USA
www.mtnlightsanctuary.com

About the cover

The book cover is a collage of photos of Mountain Light Sanctuary showing the transformation of the lodge from 1995 to 2015. This is a concrete example of the power of intention and conscious creation.

My Story

My life was a wreck in 1979. I had a wife in graduate school, three small children, my marriage was on the rocks and I had just been fired from a job that I detested. 1980 dawned with my being as deep in to 'victim mentality' as one could be.

As I frantically sought a way to keep the family together financially, I explored all kinds of options – including a multi-level marketing 'opportunity' that promised health, wealth, eternal happiness – and lots of soap...

Well, I didn't get rich and I had a lot of cleaning products in my garage for several years thereafter – not quite the success I had envisioned. But the experience did start me on a path that ultimately turned my life around.

The friend who introduced me to the business hosted weekly meetings at this home. He wasn't a poor man talking success. He was a wealthy & successful entrepreneur, and thus very believable. The weekly meetings were basically pep talks that included a lot of teachings about attitudes and beliefs, as well as some important manifestation techniques.

I'm a slow learner so it took a while, but there was a turn around. My marriage did survive and being booted out of my job was the best thing that could have ever happened. It launched me into a life of self-responsibility and social entrepreneurship that has allowed me to express my creative energies in the world, help others, and truly enjoy the adventure of life.

But lets back up...
The very first manifestation technique I learned, back in 1980, was to put up pictures of whatever I wanted in places where I would see them all the time. I learned later that this is what we now call a vision board or a treasure map. I did this and was utterly amazed over the years to see how many of those early intentions materialized, often with no effort on my part other than putting up the pictures.

The second thing I learned about manifestation was to "fake it 'til you make it" – that it is important to act as if your desires or intentions have already been fulfilled and you have become the person or have the things you have dreamed of. That was a hard one for me. I was just too honest. On the other hand, I have an alter ego hidden deep inside that is a frustrated actor wanting to come out. So I knew that I could 'play act' as long as I didn't deceive.

It started out simply. When anyone ask me "how are you doing," my response was "Great!" Now in the beginning I certainly didn't feel great. In fact I was very miserable at that point in my life. I felt like a little kid trying to walk in his dad's shoes. But over time, I changed and grew and within a few months I was actually feeling great as a result of constantly saying it. It took a while for my consciousness and self image to catch up with my words and I often felt like a hypocrite during those early days.

Along with the techniques, I was learning the importance of self-responsibility and how I had so completely disempowered myself in the past with my victim mentality and blaming others in my life for various situations and circumstances. I began to notice that, as my attitude changed, my life changed.

But like I said, I'm a slow learner. I didn't do a lot with any of this then for several years. The pictures that I had put up on the side of my refrigerator all materialized over the years, usually without overt effort and often magically, but I didn't work with any systematic vision or goals. I just floated along like most other people, taking things as they come.

Then, in the spring of 1995 I found a piece of land that I really wanted – a place to build the little cabin in the forest that I had always dreamed of. This prompted me to reemploy some techniques I had learned 15 years earlier. The first thing I did was create a vision board with photos of the land. The second thing I did was have a small stone from the creek adjacent to the land wire wrapped and wore as a necklace, next to my heart. The third thing was to write a 'manifestation letter' in the spring of 1995.

The idea is to write a letter to an old friend who you haven't seen in years and bring them up to date on your life. You begin the letter at some point in the past and continue on through the present and into the future as if everything has already occurred. So I wrote this letter to my friend and described to her in detail my purchasing the land and gave her a verbal tour through my cabin, explaining everything in detail.

Honestly at the time it felt like a complete fantasy. The land wasn't for sale. I didn't have any money for a down payment and nothing more than the modest rent I was paying to use for a monthly mortgage. Six months later, in October 1995, through a series of unpredictable occurrences, I had the land and a house. OK, it wasn't the piece of land I had initially wanted. It was an adjacent piece that, in many ways was better. I had no way to predict originally how it would all materialize from a 3D perspective. I simply created my vision board wrote my letter and held the intention.

That was 20 years ago. I've learned a lot more since then that has helped me refine this process. The first thing is the importance of Intentions. Everything begins with intention and I've come to realize from personal experience that unfulfilled dreams are often the result of unclear, unfocused or conflicting intentions. Until we are crystal clear as to what we want and have removed any blocks to it's flow, the Universe cannot provide.

The second thing I have learned is the importance of Gratitude. First and foremost is to have gratitude for what we have; being grateful for the pleasant things that make our lives better and gratitude for the unpleasant things which help us learn and grow. And then there is gratitude for the things we are in the process of manifesting as if they were already here.

So now I have embarked on a new creative phase of life. I am no longer in the 'pursuit of happiness' through the realization of dreams because I know that my happiness doesn't depend on outer circumstances of what other people do or don't do. Happiness is an inside job.

At this point in my life I do have a lot of creative dreams but I'm more like a child at the sea shore – building with the wet sand for the pure joy of creating – knowing that in the great cosmic scheme of things, it's not ultimately important and even when and where I successfully materialize a dream, the next tide will soon wash it away. So, while I give my heart and soul to the creative process, I stay lightly attached to the outcome.

And What About You?

Are You Living By Default or Design? The ancient mystics taught that our circumstances and experience in life are in fact nothing more than a mirror of our beliefs; both personal and collective. Quantum physics is now proving the truth of this, showing with scientific experiments, that we live in an interconnected holographic universe of our own creation.

This is both the good news and the bad news. The bad news is that we can no longer have the luxury of playing the victim since at the deepest levels we are participants in creating our experience. Now this isn't easy to swallow when you are facing desperate challenges that definitely look like someone else's fault; a family member, spouse, friend, colleague, a group of people or the government. But this is also the good news. If we are creators then we can change the circumstances and situations which seem to imprison us. The only question is how?

There is an equally ancient philosophy that teaches that all circumstances are essentially neutral and that it is the meaning we give them, based on our preconceived beliefs that cause us to be angry, happy, frustrated or...

Now if these two ideas are true and if we are responsible for our reality, why is it that so many people are so unhappy? It is because 999.99% of the people of the world live by default and not by design. We wake up, go to work, do what is expected of us, day after day after day until one day, when we are old, we look back and wonder where the days went and what it was all about. That is the result of living by default.

Living by design is just the opposite. It is living with meaning, purpose and passion; knowing where you want to go in life and how to get there. That is the purpose of this book; to aid you on that journey with a step-by-step program designed to help you figure out where you want to go in life and how to get there.

But it isn't for everyone....

If you are already in the perfect relationship, have all the money you need, are in great health, feel wonderful about yourself, are living in harmony with family, friends and co-workers, have the ideal job or business and have just about all the joy in life you can handle, then you can ignore the rest of this. If you are like the rest of us, you may want to read on...

Perhaps you have read "The Secret" and know that we are powerful creators beyond our wildest imaginations. The problem is this; most of our creations are unconscious and usually the result of focusing on what we don't want rather than what we do want.

The real secret is to learn how to consciously create what we really want in life rather than continually creating unconsciously what we don't want. This is true for us individually as well as humanity as a whole.

How do we do this? First and foremost, we need to learn and understand how the Universe works; Universal laws. Secondly we need to know how to consciously & deliberately apply these to our own lives rather than simply allowing life to happen to us. That's what this book is all about: to help you learn how to become a master of the situations and circumstances of life.

There is another reason that this book isn't for everyone. It requires work. Now I will admit that I have never been fond of 'workbooks' that actually require you to 'do' something. I would much prefer to read and think about a subject rather than engage in activities that require me to actually do something. But the process of conscious creation requires both 'thinking about' and concrete action.

So you will find a set of set of seven exercise which will lead you step by step through the process of setting intentions and utilizing techniques for their manifestation.

The last section of the book is an extensive annotated bibliography of books related to the various aspects of conscious creation which you use to further hone your manifestation skills.

The Purpose Of These Exercises

The purpose of these assignments is to help you understand where you are at this point in your life; the decisions and actions that brought you to this point; where you want to go in life and what you need to do to get there. The idea is to learn how to move forward consciously from this point in creating the kind of future you desire for yourself. This is done in four stages.

#1. To help you clarify where you are at this point in your life and the decisions and actions you have taken in the past that have created your situation and circumstances today. By becoming aware of this you will be able to more consciously make those decisions and take those actions in the present that will help you create the future that you want.

#2. To help you clarify your goals in life. This is done through a process of 'pivoting.' First you identify what you are dissatisfied with in life and then you 'pivot' these around to identify and determine what you do want. These become your goals.

#3. Action plan. Once you determine what your goals are, then it is a matter of prioritizing them and creating a framework for attaining them. This includes setting a time frame and understanding the resources you will need and the action steps you must take to accomplish these goals.

#4. Implementation. The last step provides you with the technique that taps the power of your creative mind & spirit. One of the things that you will find over and over again in all of the books on the Law of Attraction is the importance of visualization and imagination; the fact that it is vitally important

to see your goals - not as something to accomplish in the future –
but as if you have already reached them.

Once you have completed the written exercises you will have
laid the foundation for making your dreams come true

The books in the bibliography are divided into two sections.
Section one deals with core teachings related to conscious
creation. These include Attitudes and Beliefs, the Law of
Attraction, Intentions, Goals, Gratitude, Treasure Mapping and
Journaling. These books, along with the practical written
exercises, will give you the foundation for consciously creating
what you want in life. The second section deals with the primary
areas of life that most people what to master, such as
relationships, finances, health and emotions. The principles &
techniques in these two sections will show you how to bring
your dreams into reality.

So what do you really want?
The three primary issues that most people struggle with are
usually related in some way to finances, relationships and health.
For this reason, the bibliography includes a comprehensive list
of reading options in those areas, offering you the option of
choosing those books which speak most directly to your
personal concerns.

Lets start with Attitudes & Beliefs. There is one important
element missing in most law-of-attraction teachings. *You can
only attract into your life what you believe you can have and this is
based on your beliefs about yourself and the world.*

Compare it to a pipeline that comes from a large reservoir. The
amount of water is virtually limitless, but how much you can
receive depends on two things; the size of the pipeline and
whether it is free of blocks. Are you working with a ¼ inch pipe
or a 6 inch pipe? Are there any blocks in your pipeline that
would interrupt or divert the flow?

It is our beliefs that determine the size of our pipeline as well as the blocks which might prevent the flow. So before we get into the specific techniques of manifestation, it is important to make sure our pipe is large and clear enough to provide what we want. That's what the first few books are designed to do.

But let's begin at the beginning. Before we look at our attitudes and beliefs, we need to jump start our ability to dream big and remember the vital role our thoughts play in determining our circumstances in life. That's what the first two small introductory books are designed to do.

The second step is to set the stage. What do you really want? Until you know this, the rest is really meaningless. That's what the exercise are designed to do.

What does success look like?

If you are just starting out you may think it is the perfect relationship, job, house, car, bank account, etc. But the truth is it isn't really about any of these. The only criteria for success is your ability to master the situations and circumstances in your life and to make your dreams come true. How long will it take for you to become a master of the situations and circumstances in you life? No one can answer that except you. In many ways this is a life long journey. Your commitment to your own journey will be the only thing that will keep you going and your success in mastering the important areas of your life will be your "degree."

Introduction to the Exercises

By purchasing this book you have either made the decision to live your life by design or are at least flirting with the idea of transcending the ordinary. By doing so you have joined a small but elite group of people who are living with conscious intention. These exercises are designed to provide you with the tools to hone your skills in designing the life you want.

It is very important to take your time in completing the exercises. A great deal of thought should go into them. It is suggested that you complete a exercise, set it aside for a week or so, and then come back to it and edit it as necessary. A valuable part of the exercise is the thought that goes into it. It is also important to be completely candid in what you share. You will only benefit to the extent of your honesty.

At the end of the assignments there is an addendum with information about goals and goal setting. It is important to read this carefully and review it often.

Before you begin, It is good to read over each of the exercises and give some thought to them. Let them simmer or marinate in your mind for a while if necessary before you begin, but don't let this be an excuse for not getting started. So here we go...

Exercise #1   Study Plan
Before you begin a journey, it is important to have a map; to know where you are going, how to get there and when you expect to arrive. Read over each of the assignments below and then decide when you plan to complete each assignment. Make a list of the assignments followed by the targeted completion date. This study plan will help you stay on course and give you a set of goals to keep you on track.

Study Plan	Completion Date
Exercise #1	_____
Exercise #2	_____
Exercise #3	_____
Exercise #4	_____
Exercise #5	_____
Exercise #6	_____
Exercise #7	_____

Exercise #2   *Where Are You Now?*

Assignment #1   Levels Of Satisfaction
It is important to understand where you currently are as a starting point for knowing where you want to go and how to get there. This begins with an assessment of what you are satisfied and dissatisfied with in your life. Below are seven categories indicating levels of satisfaction. Below that are seventeen 'life areas'. Take each one of these 'life areas' and put in one of the satisfaction columns. Feel free to add other life areas that are important to you but are not included.

Completely Dissatisfied

Dissatisfied

A little dissatisfied

Neutral

A little satisfied

Satisfied

Completely satisfied

Life Areas
* Family
* Health / fitness
* Physical appearance
* Career
* Personal growth
* Educational / Mental
* Travel
* Social / Cultural
* Service & Charitable
* Romance
* Personality traits
* Recreational / Leisure

* Financial
* Spiritual / Ethical
* Material possession (houses, cars)
* Relationships
* Habits or behavior

Assignment #2   What's Working; What's Not

From the list above, choose at least seven areas that are currently important to you and write a paragraph on what's working and what's not working - or what you are happy and unhappy with in that area of your life. Feel free to share any other reflections you may have about any of these areas. You may choose more than seven areas if you wish, as long as they are important areas in which you wish to see improvement.

Assignment #3   What's Really Important?

The following questions will help you to delve deep into your own life to discover and clarify what you really value and what you want to accomplish in life at this moment. Take the time you need to answer each of these questions fully. At the end of the exercise you should have a clear map of where you really want to go in life. It is recommended that you read over all of the questions and sit with them for a while before answering.

What Brings You The Greatest Joy?

- What do you really love to do?
- What activity really makes your heart sing?
- What activities give you the greatest sense of meaning and purpose in life?
- What gives you the greatest feeling of value, importance and satisfaction?

What Are Your Greatest Concerns or Frustrations?

- What are your three most pressing problems or worries right now?
- What is the ideal solution to each of these challenges?
- How could you eliminate these problems or worries immediately?

- What is the fastest and most direct way to solve each of these problems?

What Do You Really Value?
- If you were granted three wishes, what would they be?
- If you won 100 million dollars cash, what would you do with it?
- What would you do if you had only six months to live?
- How would you define "Success" for you personally?
- What is your main goal in life at this moment?
- What is your main purpose in life at this moment?

Assignment #4   Four Questions
Think through each question carefully before you answer it. This should be done in an essay discussion format with a minimum of 500 words for each question.

A. What are my greatest strengths?
B. What are my greatest weaknesses?
C. What has been my greatest disappointment?
D. What has been my greatest accomplishment in life so far?

Exercise #3   How Did You Get Here?
Now that you are clear about what is and isn't working in your life; what you are happy and unhappy with and what is really important to you, let's take a look at how you got here. If you can understand how your decisions and actions in the past have created your current circumstances in life, then you will be able to more consciously make those decisions and take those actions now which will create the kind of future you desire.

Assignment #1   Past decisions
Review the categories in your 'dissatisfied' lists above and think about the decisions you made that may have led to this dissatisfaction. Now imagine you are being given an opportunity to live your life over again and write a long letter, as if to a trusted fried, describing how you would have proceeded differently in various situations in making certain important decisions and choices in a different manner.

Consider the several aspects of your life such as your family, career, relationships, education, personal development, etc. Be absolutely frank and consider that it is being written in strict confidence. Please remember, this is about decisions that you made, not about the circumstances of your family, childhood or youth that you had no control over. Min.1,500 words

Exercise #4   Where Do You Want To Go?
The most successful people in life are those who are able to visualize the future as if it has already happened. We call this 'back from the future thinking." These exercises help you to get specific as to what you want and begin to create a mental picture of your goals as if they were already accomplished.

Assignment #1   Your Ideal Self
The following includes four primary areas of life that most people want to change. If any area is not a priority for you, feel free to skip it. Likewise feel free to add an area that is important and ask the same questions.

Project forward five or ten years from now and imagine that your life is perfect in every respect? Now look back to where you are today and ask yourself this question: What would have to have happened for me to have created my perfect future? Write one or more paragraphs for each category, incorporating the questions below as a guide. This should be an essay format, not simply answering the questions.

Business or Career
Imagine yourself five or ten years from now. Your business or career life is perfect.
- What does it look like?
- What are you doing on an average day?
- Where is it taking place?
- Who are the kind of people you are working with?
- What level of responsibility do you have?
- What kinds of skills and abilities have you acquired in the past five years?

- How do you feel about your work? How would you describe your level of satisfaction?

Financial
Now idealize your perfect financial life. Choose either five or ten years in the future.
- How much are you earning?
- What kind of lifestyle do you have?
- Describe the house you are living in?
- What kind of car are you driving?
- What kind of material luxuries have you provided for yourself and your family?
- How much money do you have in the bank?
- How much are you saving and/or investing each month or year?

Relationships
Idealize your perfect relationships five years from now. These might include any or all of the following: family, a significant other, business partner, coworkers, friends, etc. What would these relationships look like if they were perfect in every respect.
- What does your perfect relationship with your significant other look like?
- What does your perfect relationship with your children look like?
- What does your perfect relationship with your parents look like?
- What does your perfect relationship with your siblings look like?
- What does your perfect relationship with former friends or lovers look like?
- What does your perfect relationship look like with other important people in your life?

Health and Fitness
Idealize your perfect health and level of fitness. What does it look like five years from now?

- You are in perfect physical health. Describe how you look and feel.
- How are you different now as compared to five years ago when you set your goal?
- What is your weight now that you have achieved your ideal?
- How much do you exercise each week in this ideal state and what form does it take?

Other Important Areas Of Life?
Here are some other important areas of life. Feel free to apply this exercise to any of these areas that are equally important to you.
- Habits or behavior
- Spiritual / Ethical
- Educational / Mental
- Social / Cultural
- Travel
- Service & Charitable
- Recreational / Leisure
- Personal growth
- Material (houses, cars, etc.)

Assignment #2   Setting Goals
What Is A Goal?
A goal is an end toward which you direct specific effort. This definition shows that there's an accomplishment to be achieved. The outcome is measurable, and there's a date and time of accomplishment.

Why Are Goals Important?
A person without goals is a boat without a rudder or sail. It has no direction. A person who has goals but hasn't written them down is like a boat with a rudder and a sail that has not been unfurled. A person with written goals is like a ship with the sails unfurled and speeding forward.

Goals Are Important Because:
- They give us direction
- They serve as a yardstick of progress
- They crystallize thought and clear thought motivates action
- They serve as a reminder; as a "kick in the pants."
- They help us to always know where we are, where we are going, and what to do next.
- They give us clear pictures in our mind and help us to stimulate visualization
- They focus our attention on what we want, and what we focus on we attract to ourselves.

The PPM Formula
In writing your goals, it is important to remember the 'PPPM' formula. Your goals should be positive, present, personal and measurable.

Positive
It is very important to state you goal in a positive manner. For example, you would say, "I am weighing 140 lbs. by April 1st" rather than "I want to lose 20 lbs." In other words, focus on what you want and not on what you don't want.

Present
State you goal in the present tense, as if it is already accomplished. For example, you would say, "I am totally free of tobacco on April 1st" rather than "I want to stop smoking."

Personal
Your goal must be your own and not something that someone else wants you to be, do or have. Personalize your goal by always starting it with "I" followed by a verb. For example "I am losing weight at the rate of 3 lbs. per week toward my goal of 140lbs on April 1st."

Measurable
Your goal must be measurable for you to determine whether you have reached it or not. The goals in the three P's above are all

specific and measurable. A non-specific and non-measurable goal would be something like "I want to lose weight." This can be challenging with "Being" goals (see below) but even with these you can create criteria to help you measure your progress.

The difference between a wish and a goal is having a target date when you intend to reach your goal. This requires a commitment to yourself. You may or may not reach it but you can guarantee that you won't reach it if you don't have it. Would never begin a journey to another destination without having decided when you intend to arrive. So putting down a target date is critical to the goal setting process.

Three Kinds Of Goals
As you think about choosing your goals it would also be good to realize that they fall into three basic categories: Being, Doing & Having.

'Being' Goals
These are goals related to your personality or personal characteristics. This might include being more loving, honest, enthusiastic, caring, relaxed, responsible, open, courageous, spiritual, etc. For purposes of measurement you might translate these in to specific actions or 'doing' goals.

'Doing' Goals
These are related to what you want to do and require action. This might include such things as starting a new business or service project, improving your education, getting married, changing a particular habit, changing your physical appearance, financial, etc.

'Having' Goals
These generally relate to possessions such as having a home, a specific income, a degree, etc. They are generally the end result of meeting your doing goals.

Some Additional Things to Consider
One of the most difficult challenges most people have with goals is being specific. This is because some goals are more tangible than others. Here is an example.

Tangible
- To complete my BA degree by the year 2012
- To be earning (amount) a month by January 1st 2012
- To own my own G4 Apple Macintosh laptop computer by November 20, 2012
- To visit England, France & Germany in the summer of 2012

Intangible
- To become more loving with my family and friends
- To be more firm in setting personal boundaries
- To become more frugal in handling my financial resources

From Intangible to Tangible
It is possible to translate intangible goals into tangible actions. Take for example the third sample. Your goal might be to become more frugal. A specific measurable action/goal might be "To create a monthly budget and adhere it to it."

When working with goals, it is very helpful to be clear in your own mind as to whether you are working with a tangible or intangible goal, since this will determine the kind of action plan you will build.

Another way to look at goals is whether they are performance or outcome based. You will obviously have more control over performance goals than outcome goals though outcome goals will give you a better framework for getting to where you want to go. Often you can see the outcome as the true goal and the performance goals as the action steps leading to the fulfillment of the goal. Here are some examples:

Outcome
Goal: To complete _____ studies by (date)
Goal; To obtain a bachelors degree by (date)
Goal: To obtain a scholarship for my education by (date)

Performance
Goal: To spend 5 hours a week on my ____ studies
Goal: To research at least 10 potential universities to attend.
Goal: To complete 7 educational scholarship applications by (date)

In stating goals, there are several common traps that students fall into. These include:

* Not being specific
* Not being concise
* Not being clear

Be Specific
If it is a tangible goal, then it should be specific enough to be measurable. It should include numbers, dates, or anything else by which success can be measured. State you goal beginning with the word 'to' followed by the action you will take (to obtain, to buy, to earn, etc.). Your goal or action should be stated in such a way that it will be clear to you once you have reached it.

Be Clear & Concise
Long sentences or explanations are not necessary. A simple statement such as the ones below are sufficient.

Here are examples of correct and incorrect goal statements. As you can see, the correct ones are very specific and concise. Also, they include strong action verbs such as obtain, earn, visit, submit. The incorrect set is more vague and include vague or week verbs such as want, like, need, find, decide.

Incorrect:
Goal: I want to improve my education
Goal: I would like to find some way to increase my income

Goal: I need to decide on ways to pay for my education
Goal: I plan to find a means to be able to travel more
Goal: I will decide on five schools to make application to.

Correct:
Goal: To obtain a masters degree in (subject) by (date)
Goal: To be earning (amount) each month by (date)
Goal: To obtain a scholarship by (date)
Goal: To visit Europe in the summer of (date)
Goal: To submit applications to five universities by (date)

Here are some vital questions you should ask yourself about each of your goals and actions before you turn your assignment in:

1. Is this goal tangible or intangible?
2. Is this a performance or an outcome goal?
3. Is it a short term (days, weeks, months) or a long term (years) goal?
4. Is it realistic enough to inspire me or so big as to discourage me?
5. Is the goal stated in a specific, clear and concise manner?
6. If it is tangible is it specific enough to be measurable?
7. Does it include specific criteria by which success can be measured?
8. Is the target date I stated realistic, given my current circumstances?
9. Can I picture in my mind what the accomplishment of this goal looks like?

Action Steps are specific actions you will take to fulfill your goal. These are things you will DO. They are usually specific actions with measurable results. Lets take this example.

"I will be more loving with family and friends."

This is a goal, not an action step. Action steps to fulfill this goal might be:

- I will spend 1 hour a week just doing helpful things for my (spouse, parents, etc.)
- I will spend at least 3 hours a week with my children doing what they want to do.
- I will make a list of at least 10 things I most like about my spouse, parent, etc., and tell them how I feel. These are specific action steps which you can do by specific target dates.

Now, based on your answers in exercise #4 and using the list below as a category guide, choose your top seven goals at this moment in your life and list them according to priority. Do not list the categories below. They are only a category guide from which you can choose specific measurable goals with target dates for accomplishment.

Goal #1 _____

I Intend to Accomplish this By (Date) _____

Action steps & target dates.
1. _____ _____
2. _____ _____
3. _____ _____

Goal #2 _____

I Intend to Accomplish this By (Date) _____

Action steps & target dates.
1. _____ _____
2. _____ _____
3. _____ _____

Goal #3 _____

I Intend to Accomplish this By (Date) _____

Action steps & target dates.

1. _____ _____
2. _____ _____
3. _____ _____

Goal #4 _____

I Intend to Accomplish this By (Date) _____

Action steps & target dates.

1. _____ _____
2. _____ _____
3. _____ _____

Goal #5 _____

I Intend to Accomplish this By (Date) _____

Action steps & target dates.

1. _____ _____
2. _____ _____
3. _____ _____

Goal   #6 _____

I Intend to Accomplish this By (Date) _____

Action steps & target dates.

1. _____ _____
2. _____ _____
3. _____ _____

Goal   #7 _____

I Intend to Accomplish this By (Date) _____

Action steps & target dates.

1. _____ _____
2. _____ _____

Categories
* Family
* Health / fitness
* Physical appearance
* Career
* Personal growth
* Educational / Mental
* Travel
* Social / Cultural
* Service & Charitable
* Romance
* Personality traits
* Recreational / Leisure
* Financial
* Spiritual / Ethical
* Material possession   (houses, cars, etc.)
* Relationships
* Habits or behavior

Now review each of your seven primary goals. Are they positive, present, personal and measurable? And remember, these goals will change over time as some are reached and others become more or less of a priority. This is simply a starting point to familiarize you with the process. Once you have learned it, you can overhaul your goals on a regular basis, based on the priorities in your life at the time..

Exercise #5 How Do You Get there?
Now that you know exactly where you want to go, let's take a look at how to get there.

Assignment #1   **Setting The Frequency**
There are a lot of things that can block our progress in meeting our goals. Several of these are discussed below. It's important to confront and deal with these. However, your success in reaching your goals or mastering the law of attraction is a matter of your 'frequency' based on the law of 'like attracts like.' This is the reason we constantly emphasize focusing on what you want rather than what you don't want.

The most powerful way to shift your frequency to attract what you want in life is Gratitude. So often we only focus on what we don't want. i.e. what we don't have or what we lack. Setting goals and intentions on what we want is important but our success in manifestation is ultimately dependent on the frequency we carry. We attract to ourselves those things that are consistent with our frequency and the best way to shift our frequency and lay a solid foundation for positive attraction is Gratitude.
In this exercise you are invited to consider each of following areas of your life and write at least one paragraph about what you are truly grateful for. It doesn't have to be profound. It can be the simple things that you take for granted. The goal here is to create a frequency of gratitude that will attract even more and better things into your life.

Once completed it would be good to review this on a regular basis until you really feel you are living a frequency of Gratitude for all of the blessings you have in life. Some people have become so enthusiastic with this that they maintain a Gratitude Journal and make regular entries of new items.

Gratitude Categories
* Family
* Health / fitness
* Physical appearance
* Career
* Personal growth
* Educational / Mental
* Travel
* Social / Cultural
* Service & Charitable
* Romance
* Personality traits
* Recreational / Leisure
* Financial
* Spiritual / Ethical
* Material possession (houses, cars, etc.)
* Relationships
* Habits or behavior

Assignment #2   From Goals To Intentions

Having goals is an important part of our life. Goals however, are based on some future outcome and require planning and discipline to achieve them. When you begin setting goals you start out on a journey of prioritizing and organizing the direction of your life so as to create a road map for your life.

This is an important step in becoming a master of the situations and circumstances of life. However, too often your goals become contaminated with doubts and fears as to whether they can be achieved or really lead to happiness.

Intentions, on the other hand, are not so much focused on the future but more connected to the present and how we are 'being' in any given moment. Goals are a destination and intentions are like the vehicle or perhaps the fuel. They create the momentum to move us forward toward our goals. They are based on what matters most to us bringing our actions in line with our values. Intentions flow from the heart and create your vision, while goals are created in the mind.

Goals help you with direction and taking action. Intentions are supported by your integrity and provide cohesiveness in your life. By mindfully creating your intention, you discover how to use goals that move you into action without becoming attached to the outcome. So, if you do not attain the goal that you set out to do, you can re-connect with your intentions that have no bearing on the attainment of your goals, but exist rather as the main fuel to living your life. By practicing this you become more effective in reaching your goals

Setting Intentions

The very first step in the manifestation process is being very clear as to what you want and then setting your intention. An intention is different than a wish, dream, desire or even a goal. None of these indicate the depth of commitment that an intention does, and it is our personal clarity and commitment that activates universal energies on our behalf. So first and foremost you must be clear about what you want and turn that into an intention.

You have already done this with the seven priority goals you selected in Exercise #4, assignment #2. Using this list, create a clear and concise intention, followed by a gratitude statement, a list of action steps you need to take toward manifesting this intention and a visual representation of the intention that can really excite you. Here is an example related to health.

Radiant Health (Intention)

I intend to take especially good care of my physical body without being obsessed with it. Through a good program of physical exercise, good nutrition, low stress levels, new technologies & youthful attitude - and yes, some pampering - I will maintain radiant health, a high degree of energy, a sense of well being and continual rejuvenation.

Once you have set your intentions, you are ready to Take the next step; expressing gratitude to Source or Divine Presence for it having already been accomplished. Here is an example related, also related to health.

Radiant Health (Gratitude)

I am so incredibly grateful for the vibrant health and sense of well being that I enjoy. Each day I am grateful for waking up to a new day of life and opportunity; Each day I am grateful for my body; the ability to see, hear, walk, feel, think clearly and to be free of any pain whatsoever - all the wondrous physical gifts that so many do not enjoy. I am so grateful for this physical vehicle and how it serves me day in and day out in so many different ways.

Once you have set your intention and stated your gratitude for it having already been accomplished, you may realize that you will need to take specific actions that you can actually put on your "to do" list. Here is an example

Radiant Health (Action)

- *This week I will resume my daily exercise each morning.*
- *This week I will resume my daily yoga practice*
- *This week I will resume my daily walks (run, etc.)*

- *This week I will do quite well without (caffeine drinks, tobacco, alcohol, etc.).*
- *Other actions you can begin will improve your health?*

Radiant Health (Visual)

OK, this is the fun part. Go to google.com, key in your intention, click 'images' and scroll through until you find an image that represents this intention to you - one that can really excite you. It is important to note here that it isn't so important that the image accurately visually reflects your intention as much as it emotionally represents what you want to manifest. In other words how if makes you feel (excitement, joy, etc.) is more important than an accurate visual representation.

Once you have done this for each of your primary intentions you will have created your own personal 'manifestation-mobile.'

Remember, this is a holistic process that requires your mental (intention), physical (actions) and emotional (gratitude and visuals) resources. Your emotions are a good measuring rod for how well you are doing. If reading your intention & gratitude statement along with seeing your visual gives you a feeling of happiness, excitement and joy then you will know that you have succeeded.

These positive emotions are very high frequency energies that will empower your dreams. The act of gratitude and the high frequency feelings that go with it are like stepping on the gas pedal of your manifestation mobile. It will cause you to zoom forward! And the visuals should give you the excited feeling of having already reached your goal.

On the other hand, If you allow fear, doubt, worry, jealously, anger or any other negative emotion creep into your process, it's like taking your foot off the gas and slamming on the brakes. It stops the process.

The same is true if you become unclear about what you want, feel you don't deserve it, feel that you are asking for too much or have conflicting desires such as a relationship verses freedom, for example. If and when these arise, simply say to yourself "CANCEL," and immediately shift your attention back to the gratitude for the intention already having been fulfilled. If you do this, you will eventually manifest your heart's desire.

Once completed, this will be your road map to conscious creation, one that you should review often. This will be the foundation of making your dreams come true. It is also something that will evolve and change with time. Feel free to edit and rewrite it periodically - monthly, quarterly, annually, according to your needs.

A Helpful Hint
If you want to really put the manifestation of your intentions on the fast track, then try this. Write your gratitude statements on index cards and for one month at least, dedicate one day to each gratitude statement. Read it when you wake up in the morning, Experience the pure joy of fulfillment of this intention throughout the day, and either in meditation time, driving in the car or for a few minutes before you fall asleep, visualize it's fulfillment as clearly as possible and 'bath' in the feeling of pure joy and excitement that this brings. Do this and the Universe will conspire with your own higher self to bring your dreams and intentions into reality.

Assignment #3 *Back From The Future*
The most effective way to manifest anything is to act as if your desire has already been fulfilled or accomplished. And the best way to do this is to be in a state of profound gratitude. This is much more powerful than asking for or saying that you need or want something, Since those words indicate you lack it and you are only reinforcing the fact that you don't have it.

You have already begun this process in the previous exercises. There many ways to 'act as if.' One of the most powerful ways to write a 'back to the future' letter. Here's how it works: You choose a date two to five years in the future. You have finally manifested the major intentions you set back in (current date).

You are writing a letter from this future date, beginning with a specific date two years prior to the current date. The first letter is to an old friend. The second letter is to the Source of your Being. Here's how it works:

Your letters should be dated two to five years in the future and your description of what has happened should begin approximately two years in the past from the current date. I personally use December 31st in both cases since it is the end of the year.

Letter To An Old Friend
There is an old and dear friend living very far away whom you have not seen for many, many years. You decide to write this friend a long letter to bring him/her up to date on your life, how you have changed and what you have accomplished in certain important areas of your life such as your finances, relationships, health, possessions, personal growth, etc., - whatever you are working to manifest.

You will want to share your feelings about your new life. Describe what you are doing theses days; something about your work, business, or something perhaps about your family or your love life, how you are serving others; don't forget to describe yourself physically, how you look, your health, etc. You may particularly want to describe some of the materials benefits which have resulted from your new financial situation' things such as your home, automobiles, leisure time activities, travel, etc.

You may also find it desirable to share with this trusted friend some of the internal growth that you have experienced both mentally, emotionally and spiritually as you have gained greater self-understanding through your personal journey to success. In other words you will want to write this letter in such as way as to give your friend a completed well-rounded and in-depth picture of yourself now that you have fulfilled your most cherished dreams.

After providing this overview, then choose only one primary intention and go into some detail in describing how things look now that this has been manifested.

Be sure to write as if it is already accomplished. Be as specific as possible. For example, if it is a material object such as a home or car, describe it in enough detail that your friend can get a clear mental picture of it. If it is a relationship; not only describe the person you have manifested into your life but the kind of relationship you have created with the person and especially those things about the relationship that bring you the greatest happiness. As you write, pay close attention to the feelings you are experiencing now that you have manifested your intention; the joy, the satisfaction and the gratitude.

You are doing several things with this exercise. First, and most importantly, you are clarifying on paper exactly what you want by describing it in detail as already accomplished. Secondly you are actually creating it at the higher frequencies where all creation begins.

Thirdly, you are empowering it with the emotions of joy and gratitude which fuel manifestation. Now set aside any doubts, resistance or blocks that may prevent it's delivery. And remember, if you send mixed signals to the Universe, you will get mixed results. Writing a letter such as this helps clarify and remove such blocks.

A final reminder: Be sure to date your letter with a specific date in the future and specify in the letter the date that you are starting with in the past.

Exercise #4   Letter to Source
Emotion is the gas that runs the manifestation-mobile - for better or worse. So it is important to act as if your goal has already been accomplished and to empower this with a sense of profound joy and gratitude. Strong emotions such as fear and anger will attract the very thing you don't want, based on the law of attraction.

Now sum it all up by writing a writing a letter of Gratitude addressed to The Universe / God Divine Presence; however you wish to imagine the Source of your being.

You begin your letter of Gratitude two years in the past, expressing your deep gratitude for all the good things that have taken place in your life and describing them individually. You can review the life areas list in exercise #1 for some ideas. Yes, you have had problems and challenges in many of those areas, but you also have so many things to be grateful for; many of which you have taken for granted.

Describe all of the things that have happened that you are grateful for - even the unpleasant things from which you have learned so much. Continue from two years until the present and continue expressing your gratitude for specific things that have taken *place over the next two to five years in the future - as if they have already happened.*

By the time you have finished you should notice a shift in your feelings and frequency. You should really be feeling good. This is important because it is this higher frequency of gratitude that will attract greater things into your life. This is the key: writing about the positive things which have happened over the next two to five years as if they have already happened and the frequency shift which this will create.

Assignment #5   Your Vision Board
As you will learn in almost all of the books related to manifestation, the single most powerful technique you can use for empowering your dreams is visualization. Our lives are largely ruled by our imaginations. The pictures we hold in our minds create physiological reactions in our bodies and often determine our actions in the world. Worry is a good example. Holding negative pictures in our mind and thoughts about 'what could happen' is a form of negative visualization. With enough intensity, the stress from worry can destroy both our physical and mental health; and all of this simply from our imagination!

That's the bad news. The good news is that we can use that same power of imagination and visualization to consciously focus on what we want (a product of our desires) rather than unconsciously focusing on what we don't want (a product of our fears). But it's important to remember, either way, the Universe and your own subconscious mind will conspire to bring your visual images into reality if you hold them long enough and with enough intensity.

This process is based on the Law Of Resonance: The Law of Resonance is that part of the Law of Attraction which states that our frequency - as projected though our thoughts, beliefs, words, emotions and the pictures we hold in our mind - will attract the very thing we focus on, whether positive or negative.

This is to say that the energy or frequency we project can only harmonize with energies that vibrate or resonate at a similar vibratory frequency, and it is this which determines and creates our physical experience.

The visual images we hold in our mind and the emotions around those images, along with our 'self-talk' are the most powerful tools we have for conscious creation.

You have already determined what you really, really, really in life and have listed these as your intentions. You have also empowered these intentions with visuals that represent each intention. Now you are ready to use these to create your vision board or treasure map.

What is a Vision Board?
A vision board (also known as a treasure map) is simply a visual representation or collage of the things that you want to have, be, or do in your life. It can be a 'hard copy' which you can create using poster or foam board with cut-out pictures, drawings and/or writing on it all of the things that you want in your life .

Having done your intentions, you already have a set of visuals that represent each of these. You can use these in two different ways. First, you can set them up as a screen saver so that they are constantly flashing across your screen when you computer is idle. Secondly, you can use a program like yahoo flickr and create a collage which you can also use as a screensaver, print out on an 8 _ x 11 page or order a larger poster which you can put on your wall. I did this and it provides me with constant visuals of my major goals. A large poster of my intentions is taped to my office wall. The one drawback to a hard copy is that as your goals are reached or your priorities change, the hard copy is more difficult to change than a computer copy.

However you do it, the important thing is that the visuals should reflect what you really, really, really want and looking at them should make you feel good - ideally filled with joy just thinking about their fulfillment.

When I first learned about this idea of visualization, it was suggested that I take two or three of my top intentions and post visuals of them everywhere: on the ceiling above my bed so they would be the first thing I saw when I woke up and the last thing I saw before I went to bed; on the bathroom mirror; on the dash board of my car, etc.

I never went that far. They actually ended up on the side of my refrigerator which was next to the door that went out to the driveway where the car was parked. So I saw them everything time I left or entered the house.

Space doesn't allow the details here but I can say that it was nothing short of miraculous how this one technique served to manifest each of those visuals over a period of month or years, and often in the strangest and most unpredictable way. This does work!!!

You can learn a lot more about vision boards from the books listed in our curriculum and from these websites below:
http://www.google.com/search?client=safari&rls=en&q=vision+board&ie=UTF-8&oe=UTF-8

Some Important Things To Remember
As you sharpen your skills of visualization, it's important to remember these four steps:

- Review your conscious intention.
- Visualize it in detail as an accomplished fact.
- Think, speak and act as if you already have it.
- Express gratitude for it's fulfillment as if it was already done.
- Take action on the ways and means to make it "physical" as they show up.

And finally
If you meditate daily, take some of that time to visualize yourself clearly and in detail as already having manifested your goal or dream. If you don't meditate, then take a few moments before you go to sleep or when you first wake up, to do the same thing. Be sure to bath in the positive emotions you experience with this. You might find it helpful to choose no more than seven goals and do one each day for a week and then repeat.

Exercise #6   Removing Roadblocks

Assignment #1   Confronting Your Fears
The biggest roadblock you are likely to face in reaching your goals is your fear. These may include the fear of failure, the fear of rejection, the fear of the unknown and even the fear of success.

There are two ways to deal with your fears; you can either avoid them or you can confront them. If you chose to avoid them, they will slip below your conscious mind and not only will they grow, but they will sabotage your self-esteem, self-confidence and self-respect in many ways, large and small.

If you want to move forward on the fast tract of manifestation, you will want to confront your fears. How do you do this? First and foremost, you need to acknowledge them. Shining the light of logic on them is a good start.

Exercise
Take a clean sheet of paper or several index cards and at the top write "What am I afraid of?" Now make a list of everything, major or minor, that you have any anxiety about. Consider the many areas of your life. Once done, prioritize your list with the biggest fear first. Now answer these three questions about your first fear:

- How does this fear hold me back in life?
- How does this fear help me or how has it helped me in the past?
- What would be my payoff for eliminating this fear?
- What action can I take today or this week, to confront or undermine this fear?

If you will do this with each of your major fears, you are on the way to eliminating them. It's especially valuable to review these weekly and at least once a week, answer question #4. What can I do this week to confront or undermine this fear?

Assignment #2   Resistance
Perhaps you have heard the saying: "whatever you resist, persists." Jesus was well aware of this universal law when he said "resist not evil" (Matt 5:39). This is based on the idea that what we resist, we actually empower or give energy to because we are focusing on what we don't want rather than what we do want. This is why the 'war on drugs' or the 'war or terror' or the war on anything else are ultimately doomed to failure. We are devoting all of our energy to what we don't want instead of what we do want.

Once you let go of the resistance, the judgment, and need to the control the situation or results, and let it be exactly as it is or isn't, then you will notice a difference in the way you feel. You will be releasing all of the negative feelings and despair around this situation which have been energetic blocks to the positive energy which can flow once again when you let go. It is this positive energy which will attract more positive results into your life.

It is also important to watch your words. How often have you said "I'm fighting a cold" or "I'm fighting the flu" or "I hate...." Our words are powerful beyond our imagination. Each statement we make, either to ourselves or others, is a command to our own subconscious mind and the Universe.

What we focus on, we attract. So it's really important to watch the statements you make to yourself; things such as "she is driving me crazy" "he is a pain in the neck" etc. etc. You get the picture. When you stop fighting against what you don't want and use that resistance energy to focus on what you do want, you will be putting your manifestation efforts on fast track.

Assignment #3   Releasing The Past

This is a big one. It's also an optional exercise, depending on whether or not you are ready for it. As you have learned, the Law of Attraction simply means 'like attracts like." It's a matter of vibration or frequency. Focusing on what you want (and the positive feeling or frequency that goes with that) will attract that in to your life. Focusing on what you don't want (and the negative feelings of fear, resentment, anger, etc.) will attract those things in to your life.

The low frequency feelings that we hold from the past create serious bocks to the conscious manifestation process. It's a frequency thing.

You may be well justified in your anger or resentment with a parent, past lover, ex-spouse, family member, friend or business partner who betrayed or in some way or abused you. However justified you may feel or be, the emotions from that experience is like a ton of baggage that you are dragging through life. The only person it is hurting is yourself. As one author said, "it is like drinking rat poison yourself and expecting the rat to die!"

That's why forgiveness is a major feature of all of the spiritual and wisdom traditions. They understood that forgiveness frees up and puts to better use the energy that is often consumed by holding grudges, harboring resentments and nursing unhealed wounds. Contrary to popular belief, forgiveness isn't about the other person. It's about freeing yourself - freeing up your own energy to move forward.

So you are at a choice point. You can choose to hang on to the resentment & anger, both of which will make your manifestation work that much more challenging; or you can choose to release them for the purpose of freeing up yourself. If you choose to consciously and honestly forgive those in your past, here are some exercises that may help.

There is a system of belief that says that we are responsible for everything we experience in life; both pleasant and unpleasant. That doesn't necessarily mean that we created the situation or circumstance in life but that the meaning we give to it causes us to be happy, unhappy or neutral. In other words, we have free will. We have the freedom to assign whatever meaning we wish to any event in our life. If you spouse or lover walks out on you there are two ways you can look at it: "Oh my God, what am I going to do now that he/she is gone?" or.... As Martin Luther King said "Free at last, Free at last. Thank God Almighty, I'm free at last." Or perhaps you can see it as the way being cleared for something much better to come into your life.

Ok, it's not always that clear or simple but it makes the point that you do have a choice as to how you view each situation in your life and what meaning you give it.

Exercise - Shifting Perspective
Chose a negative event in your past; a betrayal, abuse, rejection; anything that carries a strong emotional charge.

* Describe just the facts of what happened. No interpretation, no comment, no judgment. Simply the facts.

* Now write your interpretation of the situation, including your feelings about it.

* Now, in retrospect, look for the hidden blessings in the situation or event. Has anything positive resulted from it? Write

a positive interpretation of the experience so as to change the energy of it. Have you learned anything from this experience or situation that you can truly be grateful for?

Can you honestly now be in a place of gratitude for the event, while still recognizing that it was very painful? If so, then write a brief letter to the other person or persons involve and thank them for that experience and what you gained from it; what you have learned and how you have grown. When you have completed this - if you can honestly feel it - state plainly "I forgive you and I forgive myself for what happened."

Make this a letter of release; releasing you first from the chains of the past, but also releasing the other person. If you are successful, you should feel complete with that person and any feelings of resentment, anger or hatred will be replaced with simply a neutral feeling. The experience (s) of the past simply lose their emotional charge. You can choose to either send the letter to the other person(s) or simply burn it as an act of release. You will know whether or not you have been successful by what you feel when you think of the person. Is it resentment, gratitude or simply nothing?

If you aren't able to do the release as describe above, then here is a prior step that might help. Sometimes a situation or event was so very painful that we simply can't release it before we 'exorcise' it from our being. The best way to do this is to write a long and detailed letter to the object of your anger. Explain exactly how you feel about what happened and why. Pour out your anger and your pain in an effort to cause the other person to understand what you are feeling.

It doesn't matter if they are already dead. This isn't about them. It's about exorcising your own demons. Once you have done this (take several days if you need to), then create a small ceremony in which you burn it - releasing it into the ethers - with a small prayer for your own release. Then give yourself a few days or weeks to heal. By then you should be ready to reframe those past experiences and find such blessings as there may be.

Exercise #7   Your Legacy

Assignment #1   *Your Obituary*
Write your own obituary or eulogy to be read to your friends and family at your funeral, exactly as you would like to be remembered.

Assignment #2   *Your Personal Mission Statement*
A personal mission statement is your way of defining to the world who you are, why you are here and what your life is about. The following resources will guide you.

http://www.missionstatements.com/personal_mission_statements.html

http://www.nightingale.com/tmission_examplestatement.aspx

http://www.best-of-time-management.com/mission-statement.htm

Suggested Reading
The following list of books and their description were taken from Amazon.com, where they can be purchased.

Introductory Books

As A Man Thinketh (James Allen)
James Allen said that a person's mind is like a garden, which may be intelligently cultivated, or allowed to run wild. Either way, the garden will bring forth. You will be awed by the relevance of the author's thoughts and observations on the power of the mind, and mankind's ability to control life's outcomes by controlling what goes into it. This is a gift book that every pilgrim receives as a companion for their journey

Jonathan Livingston Seagull (Bach)

"Most gulls don't bother to learn more than the simplest facts of flight--how to get from shore to food and back again," writes author Richard Bach in this allegory about a unique bird named Jonathan Livingston Seagull. "For most gulls it is not flying that matters, but eating. For this gull, though, it was not eating that mattered, but flight." Flight is indeed the metaphor that makes the story soar. Ultimately this is a fable about the importance of seeking a higher purpose in life, even if your flock, tribe, or neighborhood finds your ambition threatening. By not compromising his higher vision, Jonathan gets the ultimate payoff: transcendence. Ultimately, he learns the meaning of love and kindness.

Attitudes & Beliefs

Psycho Cybernetics 2000 (Maltz)

Rather than relying on the Freudian approach of yielding control to the subconscious or on "will power" to change behavior, Psycho-Cybernetics (a computer term referring to the mental "steering system" that guides our attitudes, behavior and self-image) directs the intuitive and nonverbal right brain to "reprogram" the logical and verbal left brain through a six-step program that relies heavily on visualizations and affirmations.

The steps are: programming your "success mechanism," imagining success, shedding false beliefs, learning to relax, using "drug-free tranquilizers" and setting goals.
Through anecdotes, the authors show how people have improved their self-images and have realized their goals using Maltz's program. Self-quizzes are included. The book is both thoughtful and practical.

Success Through Positive Mental Attitude (W. Stone)

PMA stands for "positive mental attitude." This is the foundation that best selling author, Napoleon Hill based his teachings of motivation to millions of people who have transformed their lives for the better. Hill went from living in a log cabin to the life of a millionaire and influence as the author of internationally acclaimed best sellers and adviser to heads of state. This was all made possible by living what he taught.

Keys To Success (Napoleon Hill)

Hill's seventeen essential principles of personal achievement are expanded on in detail, with concrete advice on their use and implementation. You will learn the secrets of:

* filling your life with purpose and direction
* perfecting your personality
* fanning your creative spark
* building self-discipline
* profiting from the Golden Rule
* budgeting time and money

Real Magic - Creating Miracles In Everyday Life (Dyer)

"Real magic," according to Dyer, has nothing to do with sorcerers or fairy godmothers. It occurs in our daily lives when we let go of negativity and self-limiting beliefs about ourselves and our circumstances and instead pursue "perfect equilibrium of the mind."

Urging readers to "realign" themselves with the "invisible world," Dyer offers concrete suggestions about how to "get to purpose" through service to others and unconditional love, how to become spiritual beings and how to create a "miracle mindset." He also explores ways readers might improve relationships and find prosperity, personal identity and even physical health.

Finally, he explains how "real magic" can be plumbed on the global level to alleviate world problems. With anecdotes from his personal life, Dyer illustrates his own "magnificent transformation," testifying that "real magic" has led him to the higher awareness he cheers his readers toward.

The 7 Habits of Highly Effective People (Stephen Covey)

In The 7 Habits of Highly Effective People, author Stephen R.

Covey presents a holistic, integrated, principle-centered approach for solving personal and professional problems. With penetrating insights and pointed anecdotes, Covey reveals a step-by-step pathway for living with fairness, integrity, service, and human dignity -- principles that give us the security to adapt to change and the wisdom and power to take advantage of the opportunities that change creates.

Maximum Achievement (Brian Tracy)

In Maximum Achievement, Tracy gives you a powerful, proven system -- based on twenty-five years of research and practice -- that you can apply immediately to get better results in every area of your life. You learn ideas, concepts, and methods used by high-achieving people in every field everywhere. You learn how to unlock your individual potential for personal greatness. You will immediately become more positive, persuasive, and powerfully focused in everything you do.

Many of the more than one million graduates of the seminar program upon which this book is based have dramatically increased their income and improved their lives in every respect. The step-by-step blueprint for success and achievement presented in these pages includes proven principles drawn from psychology, religion, philosophy, business, economics, politics, history, and metaphysics. These ideas are combined in a fast-moving, informative series of steps that will lead you to greater success than you ever imagined possible -- they can raise your self-esteem, improve personal performance, and give you complete control over every aspect of your personal and professional life.

The Success System That Never Fails (W.Stone)

What do you want most out of life? Recognition? Money? Health? Happiness? Prestige? Love? All of these things and more can be yours if you follow just a few simple rules and put to work a revolutionary new formula.

Very little separates you from success. There is small difference between you and the great people of history. Most of them achieved their greatness not because of great intellect, but because they used the latent power within them to drive themselves up to the top. And you can do it too!

How successful you are -- in any of your desires -- is simply a matter of the right mental attitude and using the easy-to-follow principles in this book. Within these pages is an amazing new concept that shows how success can be reduced to a formula -- to a system that never fails. As you read this book something wonderful will begin to happen: you will acquire new knowledge... gain experience... become inspired.

 Soon you will recognize the ingredients for success. You will wonder why you have let life hold back these riches from you. But they will be held back no longer. Soon you will be enjoying them to the fullest. Now you will be able to judge your abilities and the powerful potential within you. Now you will see how the right mental attitude will develop your own individual success system. Now you will learn how to use that success system to obtain the true riches of life.

Laws of Success (Napoleon Hill)

This is the master volume of the extraordinary work that began the career of Napoleon Hill. Originally produced by Hill in 1928 as an eight-book series, The Law of Success is now available to contemporary readers in a single edition, redesigned and reset for ease of reading.

The Law of Success is the "golden key" to Hill's thought-his complete and unabridged mind-power method for achieving your goals. After interviewing dozens of industrialists, diplomats, thought leaders, and successful people from all walks of life, the young Hill distilled what he learned into these fifteen core lessons, organized with an introductory chapter, "The Master Mind," that serves as a primer to Hill's overall philosophy. As Hill saw it, these lessons work as a "mind stimulant" that "will cause the student to organize and direct to a DEFINITE end the forces of his or her mind, thus harnessing the stupendous power which most people waste."

While future classics of Napoleon Hill would inspire millions of readers, there is no substitute for The Law of Success for everyone who wants to grasp the full range of Hill's ideas and tap their transformative power.

Think & Grow Rich (Napoleon Hill)
The bestselling success book of all time is updated and revised with contemporary ideas and examples. Think and Grow Rich has been called the "Granddaddy of All Motivational Literature." It was the first book to boldly ask, "What makes a winner?"

The man who asked and listened for the answer, Napoleon Hill, is now counted in the top ranks of the world's winners himself. The most famous of all teachers of success spent "a fortune and the better part of a lifetime of effort" to produce the "Law of Success" philosophy that forms the basis of his books and that is so powerfully summarized in this one.

In the original Think and Grow Rich, published in 1937, Hill draws on stories of Andrew Carnegie, Thomas Edison, Henry Ford, and other millionaires of his generation to illustrate his principles. In the updated version, Arthur R. Pell, Ph.D., a nationally known author, lecturer, and consultant in human resources management and an expert in applying Hill's thought, deftly interweaves anecdotes of how contemporary millionaires and billionaires, such as Bill Gates, Mary Kay Ash, Dave Thomas, and Sir John Templeton, achieved their wealth. Outmoded or arcane terminology and examples are faithfully refreshed to preclude any stumbling blocks to a new generation of readers.

Unlimited Power (Anthony Robbins)
If you have ever dreamed of a better life, Unlimited Power will show you how to achieve the extraordinary quality of life you desire and deserve, and how to master your personal and professional life.

Anthony Robbins has proven to millions through his books, tapes, and seminars that by harnessing the power of the mind you can do, have, achieve anything you want for your life. He has shown heads of state, royalty, Olympic and professional athletes, movie stars, and children how to achieve. With Unlimited Power, he passionately and eloquently reveals the science of personal achievement and teaches you:

- How to find out what you really want
- The Seven Lies of Success
- How to reprogram your mind in minutes to eliminate fears and phobias
- The secret of creating instant rapport with anyone you meet
- How to duplicate the success of others
- The Five Keys to Wealth and Happiness

Zero Limits (Joe Vitale)
Are you overworked and overstressed? Are you doing your best but finding professional success and personal fulfillment frustratingly difficult to attain? If it seems like you work hard but never get anywhere, maybe the problem is something within you. Maybe the limitations holding you back come from inside you, not from the outside world.

Zero Limits presents a proven way to break through those self-imposed limitations to achieve more in life than you ever dreamed. Take it from Joe Vitale. He was once homeless. Now, he's the millionaire author of numerous bestselling books, an Internet celebrity, and an in-demand online marketing guru. What happened to create all of that success? How did he make it happen? Was it hard work, divine providence, or both? The answer may surprise you. It wasn't until he discovered the ancient Hawaiian Ho'oponopono system that he finally found truly unlimited success. Updated for modern times,

Ho'oponopono is a self-help methodology that removes the mental obstacles that block your path, freeing your mind to find new and unexpected ways to get what you want out of life. It not only works, but it works wonders--both professionally and personally. It works so well in fact, that Vitale had to share it with the world, so that others could experience the fulfillment and happiness he feels every day.

Teaming up with Dr. Ihaleakala Hew Len, master teacher of modern Ho'oponopono, Vitale shows you how to attain wealth, health, peace, and happiness. Vitale and Len walk you through the system, helping you clear your mind of subconscious blocks so that destiny and desire can take over and help you get what you truly want from life. It clears out unconsciously accepted beliefs, thoughts, and memories that you don't even know are holding you back.

Giant Steps (Anthony Robbins)
Based on the finest tools, techniques, principles, and strategies offered in Awaken the Giant Within, best-selling author and peak performance consultant Anthony Robbins offers daily inspirations and small actions -- exercises -- that will compel you to take giant steps forward in the quality of your life. From the simple power of decision-making to the more specific tools that can redefine the quality of your relationships, finances, health, and emotions, Robbins shows you how to get maximum results with a minimum investment of time.

The Art of Possibility:
Transforming Personal & Professional Life
(Rosamund Stone Zander and Benjamin Zander)
This is a lively, sensible manual for turning life's obstacles into possibilities. It includes a collection of illustrations and advice that suggests ways to change your entire outlook on life and, in the process, open up a new realm of possibility. Packed with examples of personal and professional interactions, the book presents complex ideas on perception and recognition in a readable, useable style.

Change or Die (Alan Deutschman)
Change or die. What if you were given that choice? We're talking actual life and death now. Your own life and death. What if a well-informed, trusted authority figure said you had to make

difficult and enduring changes in the way you think, feel, and act? If you didn't, your time would end soon-a lot sooner than it had to. Could you change when change mattered most?

"This is the question Alan Deutschman poses in Change or Die, which began as a sensational cover story by the same title for Fast Company. Deutschman concludes that although we all have the ability to change our behavior, we rarely ever do. In fact, the odds are nine to one that, when faced with the dire need to change, we won't.

From patients suffering from heart disease to repeat offenders in the criminal justice system to companies trapped in the mold of unsuccessful business practices, Deutschman demonstrates how anyone can achieve lasting, revolutionary change.

Change or Die is not about merely reorganizing or restructuring priorities; it's about challenging, inspiring, and helping all of us to make the dramatic transformations necessary in any aspect of life-changes that are positive, attainable, and absolutely vital.

Change the Way You See Everything (Cramer & Wasiak)
They say a picture is worth a thousand words, that perception is reality, and that a single strength can overcome a world of obstacles. These three powerful ideas converge in the breakthrough work, Change the Way You See Everything.

This brilliantly simple book on the philosophy known as Asset-Based Thinking, instill success-oriented habits in even the most die-hard cynic. Its transformational lessons--conveyed through unique photographic metaphors and inspiring stories from real people--reveal how the slightest shift in perception can lead to monumental results in both business and in life.

ABT is not just positive thinking, but rather a systematic observation of "what works." Kathryn Cramer, an acclaimed corporate consultant, and Hank Wasiak, a creative icon of the advertising industry, have produced a work that looks and works like no other business or self-help book. Change the Way You See Everything is a revolutionary approach to every aspect of life. You'll never look at the world the same way again.

Failing Forward -Turning Mistakes Into Stepping Stones For Success (John C. Maxwell)

The author of 24 books on maximizing personal and leadership potential, John C. Maxwell believes "the difference between average people and achieving people is their perception of and response to failure."

In Failing Forward, he offers inspirational advice for turning the difficulties that inevitably arise in life into stepping stones that help you reach the top. Noting that star performers are often those who aggressively push forward after encountering adversity, Maxwell shows how a variety of well-known and not-so-well-known people have forged ahead despite obstacles that could have derailed them.

Fire In The Soul: A New Psychology Of Spiritual Optimism (Joan Borysenko)

Difficult and tragic events, stresses Borysenko, need not ruin our lives. They often bear the seeds of transformational healing and spiritual awakening--if we are willing to receive them and shed old beliefs. In a collection that draws on anecdotes, therapeutic practice, ancient parables, myths and Bible stories, Borysenko guides the reader through "dark nights when our souls are on fire" and toward optimism, affirming the conviction that pain can be a catalyst for growth.

Happiness Is A Choice (Barry Neil Kaufman)

Kaufman, director of the Option Institute and author of A Land Beyond Tears, contends that if you change a belief or attitude you can change your life. A decision to pursue happiness, he claims, can improve relations with others: "We can engineer our own responses, choosing love over hate, peace over conflict and happiness over depression." The first five sections relate Kaufman's philosophy and offer stories of clients' successful changes while in therapy. Section six has short chapters detailing shortcuts to happiness. The book has a four-page bibliography and two pages of additional readings. A cut above most self-help books; recommended.

The Art of Happiness:
A Handbook for Living (The Dalai Lama)

Have you ever wondered what it would be like to sit down with the Dalai Lama and really press him about life's persistent questions? Why are so many people unhappy? How can I abjure loneliness? How can we reduce conflict? Is romantic love true love? Why do we suffer? How should we deal with unfairness and anger? How do you handle the death of a loved one? These are the conundrums that psychiatrist Howard Cutler poses to the Dalai Lama during an extended period of interviews in The Art of Happiness: A Handbook for Living.

Happy For No Reason: Seven Steps To Being Happy From The Inside Out (Marci Shimoff)

According to the World Health Organization, the year 2020 will see depression become second only to heart disease in terms of the global burden of illness, a sad state of affairs that motivational speaker Shimoff (co-author, Chicken Soup for the Woman's Soul) believes can be changed by learning to cultivate "a happiness that's beyond reasons and that's here to stay."

Inner happiness, she says, is within reach for anyone who can turn down the volume on their hectic lives and learn the 21 Happiness Habits that Shimoff has cultivated from 100 interviews with "deeply happy" people (including actress Goldie Hawn and author Elizabeth Gilbert).

Emphasizing a holistic approach, Shimoff takes into account mind, heart, body and soul in seven chapters that cover three Happiness Habits each, as well as corresponding anecdotes that "define what it means to be Happy for No Reason."

The personal stories of happy interviewees prove enlightening, and the principles they support are sound and commonsensical

("Focus on the solution," "Make peace with yourself," "Question your thoughts," "Practice forgiveness"), if not exactly groundbreaking. Exercises and quizzes give readers practical steps toward their goal, such as breathing exercises (Spring Forest Qigong) and writing assignments ("Write a letter to your Higher Power").

Your Faith Is Your Fortune (Neville Goddard)

According to Neville we are creators of our own lives. It matters not what other people do or think. Consciousness is the one and only creator of circumstances. Plus we cannot be affected by the consciousness of others. We are in total control of our lives at all times.

This may seem hard to believe, but if taken from a spiritual viewpoint it may be possible. On a spiritual level nothing we do can affect another soul or can affect us. We are all independent beings. Yet in this physical reality this does not seem to be the case. Here we are affected by hundreds of things. The government forces us to pay taxes, our bosses tell us what to do, or family members want us to do things we don't necessarily want to do. So if we view things from a purely physical viewpoint only we have very little power.

Yet it seems that if we live from our desired points we will in time get them on a physical level. We manifest our desires instantly via our imaginations at our source; the spiritual level. So we control how we Feel at all times.

When we are making a change in our life it usually has to do with wanting to change how we feel. So by living from our desired states as Neville proposes, we can control how we feel at all times and that is very important. It just takes a certain amount of time for our imagined states to affect the lower levels of spirit, like matter. At the source, Consciousness, the changes are made instantaneously.

My Own Worst Enemy:
Overcoming The 19 Ways We Defeat Ourselves
(Alan E. Nelson & John C. Maxwell)
Some people can't seem to get ahead in life even when they try
to improve relationships or situations. Alan Nelson suggests that
their setbacks result from attitudes that affect their behaviors,
whether they are aware of it or not.

My Own Worst Enemy describes nineteen ways people sabotage
their lives. Each chapter provides readers with a definition and
the dangers of a "behavitude"- behaviors that stem from
attitudes-such as guilt, living in the past, and self-sufficiency.
Nelson addresses the "why" behind such behavior and offers
solutions readers can use to begin changing their lives.

Nelson also provides self-assessment sections for readers to
estimate their own involvement in self-defeating behavior and
discussion questions for group or individual study.

This book is for all readers who want to take an honest look at
themselves, make changes, and begin living up to their potential.
It also appeals to pastors, counselors, and others who help
people on their paths to healing.

The Invisible Path To Success: Seven Steps To
Understanding & Managing The Unseen Forces Shaping
Your Life (Robert Scheinfeld)
Every day things happen to you. How much is caused by you and
how much by fate, destiny or the result of invisible forces you
know nothing about?

Finding the answers to these questions can be compared to
putting together a gigantic jigsaw puzzle. This work offers pieces
that have been missing from your puzzle. Once you add them to
the pieces you've already collected, a new picture of who you
are, why you're here, what your purpose is, and how to better
manage the unseen forces shaping your life will spring into view.

A Complaint Free World: How to Stop Complaining and Start Enjoying the Life You Always Wanted (Will Bowen)
Bowen is a minister with a very simple message: quit complaining. If you do, you'll be happier and healthier. Hence his Complaint-Free World challenge; the goal is to stop for 21 consecutive days. Why 21? That's how long it takes to break a habit, according to Bowen, who has appeared on Oprah and The Today Show discussing his challenge. And while there's no scientific proof his program works, he includes testimonials from people who've stopped their chronic carping and now lead more positive lives. As for issues that might make you complain about not complaining-e.g., how do you enact social change without first finding fault with the present situation?-Bowen points to Martin Luther King Jr. and his I-have-a-dream speech. He "did not stand on the steps of the Lincoln memorial and say, "Isn't it terrible how we're being treated...." Not to be critical ("Criticism is complaining with a sharp edge") but how could Bowen forget King's great rousing line that day: "America has given the Negro people a bad check, a check which has come back marked 'insufficient funds.' "

The Law of Attraction

The Law Of Attraction (Michael Losier)
You're already experiencing the Law of Attraction. You may not be aware of it, but a very powerful force is at work in your life. It's called the Law of Attraction and right now it's attracting people, jobs and relationships to your life--not all of them good!

This complete how-to reference book will teach you how to make the Law of Attraction work for you by helping you eliminate the unwanted from your life and filling it up with the things that give you energy, prosperity and joy. You can use the Law of Attraction to make a few changes in your life or do a complete overhaul. You'll find all the tools in this book. Discover how easy it is to use the Law of Attraction to: stop attracting things you don't want, increase wealth, find your perfect mate, clarify your goals and strategies, and locate your ideal job.

The Law Of Attraction in Action: A Down-to-Earth Guide to Transforming Your Life (Deanna Davis)

The phenomenal success of The Secret points to the great hunger for answers, hope, and change. But what if books like that seem a little too "out there" for you? Enter Deanna Davis, whose down-to-earth approach stems from her own change of heart (it happened at the Olive Garden).

In this fun, quirky, and decidedly straightforward guide, Deanna shares the science, strategy, and stories of how to create your ideal life using a universal key to success called the Law of Attraction, whether you seek health, wealth, happiness, success, or anything else, large or small.

The book blends cutting-edge research, practical techniques, and a conversational, light, funny tone to make the information both meaningful and memorable. Like a talk by your favorite college professor, it provides brilliant concepts in a down-to-earth manner-an uncommon blend of wisdom, creativity, inspiration, and practical strategies that work.

Money & The Law Of Attraction (Esther & Jerry Hicks)

This Leading Edge work by Esther and Jerry Hicks, who present the teachings of the Non-Physical consciousness Abraham, explains that the two subjects most chronically affected by the powerful Law of Attraction are financial and physical well-being.

This book will shine a spotlight on each of the most significant aspects of your life experience and then guide you to the conscious creative control of every aspect of your life, and also goes right to the heart of what most of you are probably troubled by: money and physical health. Not having enough money or not having good health puts you in the perfect position for creating more of that which you do not have. This book has been written to deliberately align you with the most powerful law in the universe-the Law of Attraction-so that you can make it work specifically for you.

Money, and the Law of Attraction is formatted in five essays:
Part I - Processing of Pivoting and Positive Aspects
Part II - Attracting Money and Manifesting Abundance
Part III - Maintaining Your Physical Well-Being
Part IV - Perspectives of Health, Weight, and Mind
Part V - Careers, as Profitable Sources of Pleasure

Also included is a free CD (excerpted from a live Abraham-Hicks workshop) that features the Art of Allowing your physical and financial well-being to come through.

Ask & It Is Given: Learning To Manifest Your Desires (Esther & Jerry Hicks)

Ask and It Is Given, which presents the teachings of the nonphysical entity Abraham, will help you learn how to manifest your desires so that you're living the joyous and fulfilling life you deserve.

As you read, you'll come to understand how your relationships, health issues, finances, career concerns, and more are influenced by the Universal laws that govern your time/space reality - and you'll discover powerful processes that will help you go with the positive flow of life.

It includes much advice on working with energy and emotions as well as specific chapters on increasing prosperity, reclaiming health, working with meditation, and clearing clutter for clarity. For those who are onboard with the "Laws of Attraction" and the "Art of Receiving" that Abraham speaks of, this could be one of those deliciously mysterious books that you can open to any page and it seems to offer the exact advice or insight you need right now

The Amazing Power of Deliberate Intent: Living The Art Of Allowing (Esther & Jerry Hicks)

This leading-edge book is about having a deliberate intent for whatever you want in life, while at the same time balancing your energy along the way. But it's important to note that the *awareness* of the need to balance your energy is much more significant than goal-setting or focusing on ultimate desires. And it is from this very important distinction that this work has come forth. As you come to understand and effectively practice the processes offered here, you will not only achieve your goals and desired outcomes more rapidly, but you'll enjoy every single step along the path even before their manifestation. As such, you'll find that the *living* of your life is an ongoing journey of joy, rather than a series of long dry spells between occasional moments of temporary satisfaction.

The Astonishing Power Of Emotions: Let Your Feelings Be Your Guide (Esther & Jerry Hicks) 256 pages

This leading-edge book will help you understand the emotions that you've been experiencing all of your life. Instead of the out-of-control, knee-jerk reactions that most people have to their ever-changing life experience, this work will put those responses into a broader context.

You'll come to understand what emotions are, what each of them means, and how to effectively utilize your new awareness of them. As you read, you'll come to appreciate, and make peace with, where you are right now, even though there is so much more that you may desire. Every thought you absorb will bring you to a greater understanding of your own personal value and will show you how to open your own doors to whatever you may wish to be, do, or have.

Law of Attraction Workbook - A 6-Step Plan to Attract Money, Love, and Happiness (David Hooper)

In this workbook, you'll learn the exact process to attracting everything you've ever wanted in life, including greater joy, excellent health, quality relationships, and unlimited money. This workbook will give you everything you need to understand the Law of Attraction. You'll get a better sense of how your relationships, health issues, finances, career concerns, and other aspects of life are influenced by this universal law. This is more than just theory... It's practical information that will work for you. Fill in the blanks to walk away with your personalized plan to apply the Law of Attraction in your life.

Jack Canfield's Key to Living the Law of Attraction: A Simple Guide to Creating the Life of Your Dreams (Jack Canfield)
Long before co-creating the bestselling Chicken Soup for the Soul series, Jack Canfield was already teaching the ancient principles of the Law of Attraction. Canfield has been consciously living in harmony with this universal law for more than thirty years, and his personal success is a testament to its power.

Now, in Jack Canfield's Key to Living the Law of Attraction, he shares his knowledge and experience with you and offers you his proven tools and techniques for applying the Law of Attraction in your own life.

This book is a simple 'how to' guide for using the Law of Attraction to create the life you desire. Within these pages, Canfield clearly explains not only what you need to know, but what you need to do in order to attract what you want in your life.

Jack Canfield's Key to Living the Law of Attraction addresses the important issues of clarity, purpose, and action. This thought-provoking guide will take you step by step through the processes of defining your dreams, goals, and desires. Along the way, you will gain a greater understanding of yourself-a sense of who you really are and why you are here. Your journey begins right here, right now. You can change your life, increase your awareness, and empower yourself to create an amazing future-one that is filled with love, joy, and abundance.

Life Lessons for Mastering the Law of Attraction: 7 Essential Ingredients for Living a Prosperous Life (Jack Canfield)
Do you ever wonder why some people always seem to be at the right place at the right time, enjoying good fortune, health, the ideal mate, happy kids, and achieve more than the average person could ever imagine? Have you wondered what makes them so 'lucky' or well connected? People who enjoy a heightened state of living and have their dreams and goals realized to their fullest potential have tapped into one of the

oldest and influential principles for living a fulfilled life--the Law of Attraction.

Life Lessons for Mastering the Law of Attraction teaches you what you need to know about living the Law of Attraction and how to create your own personal success through its concepts.. Filled with exercises, lessons, real-life stories, and proven key ingredients, Life Lessons for Mastering the Law of Attraction, from the creators of Chicken Soup for the Soul®, reveals how to master the law's basic tenets, which include: defining moments in life, creating space to create prosperity, acting 'as if,' trusting in intuition, transforming thought, having an 'attitude of gratitude,' and changing the impossible to possible. People have been using these techniques for thousands of years to attract their desires and now you too will be able to create the life of your dreams.

The Law of Attraction, Plain and Simple: Create the Extraordinary Life That You Deserve (Sonia Ricotti)
Readers of The Law of Attraction, Plain and Simple can live the life of their dreams, their "greatest life," by applying Sonia Ricotti's eleven simple steps to enjoy freedom and inner peace in every area of life. The Law of Attraction states that we attract into our lives what we project into the universe. Written in concise, plain English and filled with stories, tips, and exercises, this book helps readers shift their thoughts, language, and emotions to emit positive vibrations and attract all they want in life. Using the eleven steps in this book, readers stop projecting negative energy and learn to project positive energy at all times. The eleven steps include:

- Decide What You Want
- Choose Your Thoughts and Feelings
- Unleash the Past
- Keep the End in Mind
- Connect Mind, Body, and Spirit
- Choose Your Friends Carefully
- Allow It (allow what you attract to arrive)

With The Law of Attraction, Plain and Simple, Ricotti successfully strips away the esoterica often associated with Law of Attraction books, to present this universal law in a simple, commonsense, psychologically grounded way.

Expect Miracles (Joe Vitale)

Manifesting one's dreams and wishes is not as hard we think it is. Vitale's practical, easy to apply psychology involves attracting one's life desires by understanding and accepting them. This book enables readers to show results on their own quickly and easily. Miracles are neither impossible to experience nor difficult to achieve if we allow ourselves to make them possible.

The Law of Attraction Made Simple - Magnetize your heartfelt desires   (Jonathan Manske)

Finally, an eye-opening book packed with powerful and easy to use tips, tools and techniques to activate the Law of Attraction in your life. Become a magnet for more of what you want in your personal and professional life. Get the results you deserve. You will be amazed at how simple it is. Read and discover:

- How to powerfully attract more of what you want
- The proven five-step formula to create 'luck'
- How to work with your non-conscious mind to get measurable results
- Simple solutions to finally get out of your own way
- How to maximize your happiness and success with little known attraction secrets
- surefire method to de-hypnotize yourself from limiting beliefs and agreements
- How you prosper when you know the deeper purpose of the Law of Attraction

Born to Manifest, Law of Attraction Tools and Techniques (Thomas Murasso)

It's message has existed throughout the history of mankind. and several exceptional men and women who discovered the secret; the Law of Attraction, went on to become known as the greatest people who ever lived. Simply put, the Law of Attraction states, I attract to my life whatever I give my energy, attention and focus to...whether good or bad!

Born to Manifest explains the Law of Attraction in simple terms, and most importantly, gives you the tools to stop attracting what you don't want in your life, as well as the techniques to deliberately manifest what you do! Born to Manifest is a how-to manual for consciously creating a fantastic life for ourselves!

Placing Your Order: Steps for Creating Successful Manifestations (K. C. Craig)

Placing Your Order is designed to be a self-help book about manifesting your wants, needs and desires on this physical plane of existence, through the power of your thoughts.

Heart's Desire: Instructions For Creating The Life You Really Want (By Sonia Choquette)

There are lots of books out there on creative visualization, but Choquette, author of The Psychic Pathway (1995), offers something more. She helps readers figure out exactly what they want before they try to get what they think they want. She then goes on to show how creative manifestation is available to everyone who learns the process.

The engaging, chatty writing style might make this manual seem less serious than some books on the topic of spiritual development, but readers who undertake the step-by-step program Choquette sets out will find material that is insightful, even inspiring.

Choquette shares the nine universal principles for creating the reality of your dreams. Step by step, with practical advice, specific exercises, and modern-day parables, she teaches readers to make the changes in thought and behavior that will lead them to the attainment of their most heartfelt desires.

The Amazing Power of Deliberate Intent: Living the Art of Allowing (Jerry & Esther Hicks)

This leading-edge book by Esther and Jerry Hicks, who present the teachings of the nonphysical entity Abraham, is about having a deliberate intent for whatever you want in life, while at the same time balancing your energy along the way. But it's important to note that the awareness of the need to balance your energy is much more significant than goal-setting or focusing on ultimate desires. And it is from this very important distinction that this work has come forth.

As you come to understand and effectively practice the processes offered here, you will not only achieve your goals and desired outcomes more rapidly, but you'll enjoy every single step along the path even before their manifestation. As such, you'll find that the living of your life is an ongoing journey of joy, rather than a series of long dry spells between occasional moments of temporary satisfaction.

Living With Intention (Deanna Davis)

There is an art and a science to living deliberately. Living With Intention is about exploring your priorities and passions, and capitalizing on your skills and gifts. It's about honoring what is important to you and making purposeful choices about what you want to do next. It's about finding meaning in all you do.

Using a unique combination of information, inspiration, reflection, and action, Living With Intention guides you in creating a vision for who you want to be and how you want to design your life. In this book, you will explore six key foundations for designing a wildly fulfilling and remarkably successful life: 1) Powerful Perspectives: Create an attitude of possibility and opportunity by transforming your outlook. 2) Get Vivid, Get Busy, and Get Support: Design an inspiring vision and practical goals that ensure fulfillment and success. 3) Energy, Focus, Outcomes: Direct your time, energy, and expertise to achieve outstanding results in everything you do. 4) Enduring

Happiness: Practice the science of life satisfaction to weave more joy and contentment into your days. 5) What You Do Best: Identify your unique strengths and gifts, and use them to create the life you want. 6) Balance and Resilience: Tap into the power of positive stress while minimizing the impact of negative stress. Living With Intention takes you on a voyage toward the life you were born to live.

The Power Of Intention:
Learning To Co-create Your World Your Way (Wayne Dyer)

After years of spiritual study and reflection, inspirational speaker and bestselling author Wayne Dyer has emerged a highly esteemed teacher. His current message about tapping into the power of intention may sound like good old positive thinking: just stay focused on what you want, rather than focusing on the lack of having what you want. But the teaching here goes deeper than just controlling thoughts (although he does acknowledge that thought control is a surprisingly challenging and significant endeavor).

This book might help readers land a better job, but it's more relevant for those who are ready to detach from an ego-driven life filled with quick fixes of happiness and step into a more authentic, joyful, and spiritually fulfilling life. His core teachings speak to tapping into a universal source of energy that can also be called the "power of intention." He calls people who are consciously co-creating with this energy source "connectors" and describes them as "individuals who have made themselves available for success...They don't say With my luck things won't work out. Instead, you're more likely to hear something like, I intend to create this and I know it will work out."

The Art Of Conscious Creation (Jackie Lapin)

Are you ready to learn how to manage your personal energy frequency for the purpose of personal and global transformation? The Art of Conscious Creation gives you the simple yet extraordinary techniques to "Consciously Create" the life you yearn for and desire!

This compelling book reveals the 25 Universal Guiding Principals that lead to a happier, more fulfilling, prosperous, and struggle-free life. You will then discover how to apply these remarkably powerful skills on behalf of the planet, helping to manifest a world that is free of hate, war, rage, hunger and environmental destruction...a world instead filled with peace, prosperity, unlimited opportunity and joy for all.

Contained within this book are keys to mastering visualization on a personal and global level, to harnessing the energy that can change your life, impact the Universe and transform the world. Learn how joining with others can magnify the power of your thoughts exponentially to create a bountiful future.

The Self Aware Universe: How Consciousness Creates The Material World (Reed & Goswami)
Consciousness, not matter, is the ground of all existence, declares University of Oregon physicist Goswami, echoing the mystic sages of his native India. He holds that the universe is self-aware, and that consciousness creates the physical world.

Calling this theory "monistic idealism," he claims it is not only "the basis of all religions worldwide" but also the correct philosophy for modern science.

Once people give up the assumption that there is an objective reality independent of consciousness, the paradoxes of quantum physics are explainable, contends Goswami, writing with his wife and Reed (Building the Future from Our Past).

He also applies his hypothesis to the so-called mind-body schism, which he attempts to heal. Sketching a model of the self, this demanding but rewarding treatise uses analogies from the "new physics" to throw light on choice, free will, creativity, the unconscious and paths to spiritual growth. Illustrated.

The Intention Experiment: Using Your Thoughts To Change Your Life & The World (Lynne Taggart)

In The Intention Experiment, internationally bestselling author Lynne McTaggart, an award-winning science journalist and leading figure in the human consciousness studies community, presents a gripping scientific detective story and takes you on a mind-blowing journey to the farthest reaches of consciousness.

She profiles the colorful pioneers in intention science and works with a team of renowned scientists from around the world, including physicist Fritz-Albert Popp of the International Institute of Biophysics and Dr. Gary Schwartz, professor of psychology, medicine, and neurology at the University of Arizona, to determine the effects of focused group intention on scientifically quantifiable targets -- animal, plant, and human.

The Intention Experiment builds on the discoveries of McTaggart's first book, international bestseller The Field: The Quest for the Secret Force of the Universe, which documented discoveries that point to the existence of a quantum energy field. The Field created a picture of an interconnected universe and a scientific explanation for many of the most profound human mysteries, from alternative medicine and spiritual healing to extrasensory perception and the collective unconscious. The Intention Experiment shows you myriad ways that all this information can be incorporated into your life.

After narrating the exciting developments in the science of intention, McTaggart offers a practical program to get in touch with your own thoughts, to increase the activity and strength of your intentions, and to begin achieving real change in your life. After you've begun to realize the amazing potential of focused intention, and the times when it is most powerful, McTaggart invites you to participate in an unprecedented experiment: Using The Intention Experiment website to coordinate your involvement and track results, you and other participants around the world will focus your power of intention on specific targets, giving you the opportunity to become a part of scientific history.

Goals

Goal Mapping
How to Turn Your Dreams Into Reality (Brian Mayne)
Traditional goal-setting techniques focus on left-brain words and endless repetition to embed goals into the subconscious. Goal Mapping uses imagery, the language of the subconscious, to impact both halves of the brain, creating a potent force. The book outlines a series of simple steps to help readers open the mind and visualize dreams and aspirations, and then, using the templates provided, to map out specific goals or even a period of life. Whatever the dream, Goal Mapping can help achieve it.

Goal Setting 101 (Gary Ryan Blair) 58 pages
This book offers solid advice on setting and achieving your goals. Goal Setting 101 helps you to become brilliant on the basics by explaining the Who?, What?, Where?, When?, How?, and Why? of goal setting. You will learn what to do before, during, and after as you pursue any goal.

Goals! How to Get Everything You Want--Faster Than You Ever Thought Possible (Brian Tracy)
Based on more than 20 years of experience and 40 years of research, this book presents a practical, proven strategy for creating and meeting goals that has been used by more than 1 million people to achieve extraordinary things in life.

Author Brian Tracy explains the seven key elements of goal setting and the 12 steps necessary to set and accomplish goals of any size. Using simple language and real-life examples, Tracy shows how to do the crucial work of determining one's strengths, values, and true goals. He explains how to build the self-esteem and confidence necessary for achievement; how to overpower every problem or obstacle; how to overcome difficulties; how to respond to challenges; and how to continue moving forward no matter what happens. The book's "Mental Fitness" program of character development shows readers how to become the kind of person on the inside who can achieve any goal on the outside.

Gratitude

Gratitude: A Daily Journal (Jack Canfield)

As Jack Canfield's Key to Living the Law of Attraction explains, gratitude and acknowledgment are essential components in creating and attracting what you want in your life. Through the expression of gratitude on a daily basis, you align yourself to receive all the good the universe has to offer. By simply focusing your thoughts and attention on the abundance that is already present in your life, you will literally shift your energy to a positive vibration that will automatically and effortlessly attract even more to be grateful for.

Gratitude: A Daily Journal is a year-long, two-part journal that provides a simple framework for your personal expressions of gratitude and acknowledgment. This journal is a powerful tool that will help to raise your consciousness and increase your awareness of the beauty and synchronicity that surround you each day. With each daily expression of gratitude, you will create a vibrational match for love, joy, and abundance.

Thank You Power: Making the Science of Gratitude Work For You (Deborah Norville)

Thank You. Can such small words hold life-changing power? Yes! Rooted in science, presented from a spiritual perspective, Thank You Power details the surprising life improvements that can stem from the practice of gratitude. In this eye-opening book, Deborah Norville brings together for the first time the behavioral and psychological research that prove what people of faith have long known: giving thanks brings life blessings.

Beginning with two small words, thank you, Norville shows how anyone can be happier and more resilient, have better relationships, improved health, and less stress. After two years of scientific research, Norville brings it all together with powerful personal stories of thank you power in action and gives specific steps for readers to cultivate thank you power and put it to work in their own lives.

Thanks! How The New Science Of Gratitude Can Make You Happier (Robert Emmons)

This fine, succinct contribution to the relatively new field of positive psychology (which seeks to promote emotional wellness, rather than treat disorder) focuses on what a French saying calls the memory of the heart. Emmons (The Psychology of Gratitude), a leader in the field and professor at UC-Davis, looks at gratitude from an interdisciplinary perspective, including literature, psychology, religion and anthropology. He demonstrates how it contributes to emotional equanimity and pleasure, richer personal relationships and greater health.

Perhaps Emmons's most interesting chapter is on ingratitude, which Kant called the essence of vileness and which Emmons sees as resulting from the grudging resentment of one's own dependence on others. Gratitude is more... than a tool for self-improvement. Gratitude is a way of life Emmons says, and he ends by offering 10 ways to cultivate gratitude, including keeping a gratitude journal and learning prayers on gratitude. Emmons introduces an important topic through deftly synthesizing scientific and popular inspirational literature:

Living Life as a Thank You: The Transformative Power of Daily Gratitude (Mary Beth Sammons)

Whatever is given - even a difficult and challenging moment - is a gift. Living as if each day is a thank-you can help transform fear into courage, anger into forgiveness, isolation into belonging, and another's pain into healing. Saying thank-you every day inspires feelings of love, compassion, and hope.

These ideas are the basis for this timely book. Authors Nina Lesowitz and Mary Beth Sammons present a simple, but comprehensive program for incorporating gratitude into one's life, and reaping the many benefits that come from doing so.

The book is divided into ten chapters from "Thank You Power" and "Ways to Stay Thankful in Difficult Times" to "Gratitude as a Spiritual/Cultural Practice " and "Putting Gratitude into Action."

Each chapter includes stories of individuals whose lives have been transformed by embracing this program, along with motivating quotes and blessings, and a suggested gratitude practice such as keeping a weekly gratitude journal and starting a gratitude circle.

Count Your Blessings:
The Healing Power Of Gratitude (John F. Demartini)

Are you really living or barely breathing? Do you feel sick, run-down, anxious, or low? In Count Your Blessings, Dr. John F. Demartini reveals the connection between health and state of mind. The old adage about making the most of what you've got forms the basis of 25 principles that will help you to live a healthy and fulfilling life. Through real-life examples, exercises, meditations, and affirmations, Dr. Demartini shows how you can use and develop your own inner resources, just by living in the present moment.

- How to turn any stressful situation into an inspiring learning experience
- Transform the negativity of your fears and problems into positive actions
- Discover your goals and how to stick to them
- Learn to love what you do
- How to create more loving relationships

Count Your Blessings will be the source or inspiration you will come back to again and again.

Treasure Mapping

Goal Achievement Through Treasure Mapping
(Barbara Laporte)

Goal Achievement through Treasure Mapping: A Guide to Personal and Professional Fulfillment shows readers how to apply principles discussed in the best-selling book The Secret. Barbara Laporte helps you understand The Law of Attraction (or Law of Mind Action) and provides proof of the power of intention and visualization by telling touching, true stories of people who have manifested their goals using Treasure Mapping.

Through these success stories, you will learn ways to release negativity and clutter, appreciate the lessons of the present moment, and focus on your goals with positive expectancy. Five simple steps get you started on this fun and easy tool for transforming your life and achieving your goals. Whether your goal is a romantic relationship, a more fulfilling career, a healthier body image, or any other pure desire, you will be touched and inspired by the stories Barb tells, motivated to transform your own life, and challenged to reflect on how best to do this.

The Complete Vision Board Kit: Using the Power of Intention and Visualization to Achieve Your Dreams (John Assaraf)
A vision board is a powerful tool that anyone can use to shape an ideal future through the power of intention and visualization. Learning how to vividly imagine your desired results is the first step on the path to making them happen.

Break through unconscious, limiting beliefs and get ready to transform your future now. If you can envision it, you're halfway there! This book will explain and walk you through exactly how to create a vision board in conjunction with how to retrain your brain to actually start believing that you can achieve all your goals and dreams. Then, the universe will work its magic! This is a great personal gift and one your friends and family will love

Visioning: Ten Steps to Designing the Life of Your Dreams (Lucia Capacchione)
This how-to manual for "manifesting your heart's desire" will no doubt prompt memories of kindergarten collage-making for many readers. Based on her observations of engineers, architects and designers (including toy and theme park creators), Capacchione offers a framework for shepherding an idea into reality, whether the goal is to create a company mission statement, improve one's health or build a dream home.

An art therapist, corporate consultant and the author of 10 books (The Creative Journal, etc.), she instructs readers on choosing a theme, gathering images and words that "grab" one's attention, finding order in the chaos, committing one's vision to paper and glue, getting feedback from others, dwelling on one's vision, getting help to implement the plan and celebrating the final result.

With a tone that's both playful and serious, Capacchione provides detailed instructions and numerous exercises for working through this process. She also encourages journal writing (using both hands to engage both sides of the brain) and addresses common internal and external obstacles. Even if some of the numerous samples and stories culled from her workshops come across as a bit schematic and glib, Capacchione provides a fun and empowering approach to creativity for those willing to roll up their sleeves and play in the rich field of their desires. (Jan.)

Create your own Vision Board with Heart! (Antar Wagoner)
Growing up with severe Manic Depression and A.D.D in an abusive environment he was able to find relief and peace through prayer and positive focus using Vision Boards.

Master Vision Board creator Antar has travelled the world researching wisdom, truth and how to manifest. Now he assists people worldwide in re-creating the mind. Antar shares experiences of weight loss, wealth, healing, and repaired relationships using Biblical principles, prayer and ancient teachings. Antar is a Certified Clinical Hypnotherapist, expert in Guided Visual Imagery, he shows there is indeed hope for those suffering in the world today.

Journaling

The Many Faces of Journaling: Topics &: Techniques for Personal Journal Writing (Linda C. Senn)
This book opens with a chapter on the history of journaling with sample entries by such notables as Walt Whitman and Anne Frank. It then moves on to 12 topic chapters, such as therapeutic-cathartic writing, recording personal goals and growth, and developing your creativity. This second edition of

The Many Faces of Journaling includes two chapters: Scrapbook Journaling and Environmental Journaling, each of which is a hot topic among today's media and hobbyists. Chapters 2 - Personal Growth & Goals, 3 - Therapeutic Journaling, and 4 - Upbeat Journaling all deal with aspects of personal development. Chapters 5 - Creativity Journaling and 6 - Scrapbook Journaling are more playful. The next chapters 7 - Journaling for the Next Generation, 8 - Historic Perspective, and 9 - Environmental Journaling teach the reader effective ways to record past and current events from a personal perspective for future readers. Chapters 10 - Nature Journaling, 11 - Dream Journaling, and 12 - Travel Journaling demonstrate different methods for writing in depth about each topic. And in chapter 13 - Chronological Journaling, Senn explains how to use a daily journal for current and future reference, including such nitty gritty facts as the date on which your car gets an oil change and when you got your last tetanus shot.

In each chapter, the author describes the benefits and assorted methods of writing for each topic, shows the readers how to spice up their journal entries, and includes over 130 examples throughout the book. The Creating Fascinating Family Memoirs appendix provides a step-by-step plan for writing a family history, one person at a time. The simple family tree creates a framework from which to begin making detailed notes. The author then shows how to add life and flavor to each family member's description complete with examples.

Journalution: Journaling to Awaken Your Inner Voice, Heal Your Life and Manifest Your Dreams (Sandy Grason)

Studies confirm what avid journalers have always known: that writing about difficult experiences helps the writer move forward. Many self-help books recommend journaling as a way to express emotions and explore past hurts - as well as to simply get organized, make plans, and set goals - yet few of the books show how to do it. In Journalution, Sandy Grason combines the writing guidance of Julia Cameron with the emotional nurturing of Shakti Gawain. With chapters including "Completing Your Incompletions," "Masterminding Your Destiny," and

"Communicating with a Higher Power," the book balances basic instruction in the art of journaling with intimate entries from the author and her workshop participants. Activities, such as timed and stream-of-consciousness writing exercises and keeping a dream log, follow each chapter. Throughout, Grason offers guidelines and prompts, encouraging readers to pick up the pen and journal their way to greater self-awareness.

Writing For Emotional Balance: A Guided Journal To Help You Manage Overwhelming Emotions (Beth Jacobs)
The practice of keeping a journal is increasingly being recommended by therapists and other health care professionals as a tool for gaining a better understanding of one's life situations and corresponding emotions. In this book, Jacobs provides readers with a progressive, step-by-step guide for doing so easily and effectively. Journals, she writes, are "a checkpoint between your emotions and the world," that enable us to view our feelings from a distance, and to become clearer about the beliefs and attitudes that shape them.

Beginning with an explanation about the value of keeping a journal, Jacobs then guides readers through various processes to clarify our understanding of the subjective nature of emotions and how they are influenced by time and memory. Readers then learn how to define and evaluate their emotions, predict their emotional patterns, release emotions that no longer serve them, and refocus and organize their emotional life in ways that are more appropriate and fulfilling. Supported by over 30 hands-on exercises, this guide is an excellent resource for novice and seasoned journalists alike

When you've decided you can't take it any more, it helps a great deal to know what it actually is. The process of writing about overwhelming emotions is a remarkably effective means of creating clarity and perspective in your life. Regular journal writers and diarists rely on their writing to help them keep their emotions in perspective; this book distills the best emotional benefits of regular personal writing into a series of engaging and easy-to-practice writing exercises.

This book begins by helping readers explore why they were drawn to journaling in the first place and what their goals are for their writing experiments. Short projects help readers name their emotions, distancing them from overwhelming feelings so that they can react more constructively. Other exercises work to help readers interpret emotions from different perspectives. By learning to gauge their emotional reactions on a "feelings barometer," readers will come to understand the perceived strength of an emotion. Further exercises encourage readers to discover emotional triggers, write an emotional history, and connect physical and emotional responses. By practicing these exercises, readers will develop a language of positive imagery that will enhance comfort and peace of mind.

Journal to Self: Twenty Two Paths To Personal Growth (Kathleen Adams)

A nationally known therapist provides a powerful tool for better living--a step-by-step method to personal growth, creative expression, and career enhancement through journal writing.

Life's Companion: Journal Writing As A Spiritual Quest (Christina Baldwin)

In Life's Companion, Christina Baldwin points out that writing is a means of expanding our inner horizons, of relating more meaningfully to the world we live in and to other travelers on the spiritual path. Baldwin, a leader of the renaissance of personal writing, has taught personally more than 30,000 people the joys of journaling. The book illuminates its text with enlightening quotations, exercises, questions, and techniques to nurture the writer and seeker within. Centered in a broad spiritual philosophy, Life's Companion shows readers how to transform writing into a tool for self-growth, heightened awareness, and personal fulfillment.

Relationships

The following list of recommended books deal with relationships, starting with the most important relationship; the one you have with yourself.

What To Say When You Talk To Yourself
(Shad Helmstettter)

Your most important relationship is the one you have with yourself. What are you constantly telling yourself? This book teaches us that we literally become what we think and tell ourselves. Other books have touched on this concept in the past, but this book teaches us quick and easy methods to stop unwanted thinking/behaviour patterns - to "erase and replace" our negative thoughts with ones which will build our success.

Prior to reading this book approximately 10 years ago - this technique required many hours of written assignments and counselling. Individuals now have a simple and effective tool to make permanent positive change in their lives by learning the right things to say to themselves. This book goes beyond positive thinking, it is more than wishful thinking with no concrete instructions on how to achieve happiness. This is a quick and easy method to create any level of change you desires by using specific self-talk words and scripts throughout the day.

Nonviolent Communication:
A Language Of Life (Marshall Rosenberg)

Do you hunger for skills to improve the quality of your relationships, to deepen your sense of personal empowerment or to simply communicate more effectively? Unfortunately, for centuries our culture has taught us to think and speak in ways that can actually perpetuate conflict, internal pain and even violence.

Nonviolent Communication offers practical skills with a powerful consciousness and vocabulary to help you get what you want peacefully. Rosenberg offers insightful stories, anecdotes, practical exercises and role-plays that will dramatically change your approach to communication for the better. Discover how the language you use can strengthen your relationships, build trust, prevent conflicts and heal pain. Revolutionary, yet simple, NVC offers you the most effective tools to reduce violence and create peace in your life-one interaction at a time.

How To Win Friends & Influence People (Dale Carnegie)
This grandfather of all people-skills books was first published in 1937. It was an overnight hit, eventually selling 15 million copies. How to Win Friends and Influence People is just as useful today as it was when it was first published, because Dale Carnegie had an understanding of human nature that will never be outdated.

Financial success, Carnegie believed, is due 15 percent to professional knowledge and 85 percent to "the ability to express ideas, to assume leadership, and to arouse enthusiasm among people." He teaches these skills through underlying principles of dealing with people so that they feel important and appreciated. He also emphasizes fundamental techniques for handling people without making them feel manipulated.

Carnegie says you can make someone want to do what you want them to by seeing the situation from the other person's point of view and "arousing in the other person an eager want." You learn how to make people like you, win people over to your way of thinking, and change people without causing offense or arousing resentment. For instance, "let the other person feel that the idea is his or hers," and "talk about your own mistakes before criticizing the other person." Carnegie illustrates his points with anecdotes of historical figures, leaders of the business world, and everyday folks

Straight From
The Heart: An Essential Guide For Developing, Deepening & Renewing Your Relationship (Layne & Paul Cutright)
With this powerful new guidebook you can create the magnificent relationships you truly desire. Featuring an insightful exploration of the dynamics of your interactions with others, Straight From the Heart also provides step-by-step guidance and practical process you can do with your romantic partner, business colleagues, family members or friends.
No matter how gifted (or unpracticed) a communicator you are, each of these "Heart-to-Heart Talks" will bring you new levels of intimacy, trust and understanding. They create an atmosphere of

discovery and a fuller experience of who and what you are - both as an individual and in the context of your most important relationships. Direct, concise and immediately beneficial, this book is based on the authors' 23 years of personal and professional experience. All of the exercises were conceived in the Cutright's own romantic partnership and perfected in their successful teaching practice.

The Relationship Cure: A 5-Step Guide to Strengthening Your Marriage, Family, and Friendships (John Gottman) - John Gottman is a leading explorer of the inner world of relationships. In The Relationship Cure, he has found gold once again. This book shows how the simplest, nearly invisible gestures of care and attention hold the key to successful relationships with those we love and work with. Gottman has discovered the Rosetta Stone of relationships. He has decoded the subtle secrets contained in our moment-to-moment communications.

By introducing the simple yet amazingly powerful concept of the "bid," he provides a remarkable set of tools for relationship repair. By the middle of the second chapter you're likely to say to yourself, "Oh, so that's what's happening in my relationship with my partner (or colleague, boss, or sister), and now I know what to do about it. What distinguishes Gottman's writing from that of other self-help books is that it is based on research findings from his extensive studies. When he says his five steps will help you build better connections with the people you care about, you know that they have been demonstrated to work

You Just Don't Understand:
Men & Women In Conversation (Deborah Tannen)
Georgetown University linguistics professor Tannen here ponders gender-based differences that, she claims, define and distinguish male and female communication. Opening with the rationale that ignoring such differences is more dangerous than blissful, she asserts that for most women conversation is a way of connecting and negotiating. Thus, their parleys tend to center on expressions of and responses to feelings, or what the author

labels "rapport-talk" (private conversation). Men, on the other hand, use conversation to achieve or maintain social status; they set out to impart knowledge (termed "report-talk," or public speaking). Calling on her research into the workings of dialogue, Tannen examines the functioning of argument and interruption, and convincingly supports her case for the existence of "genderlect," contending that the better we understand it, the better our chances of bridging the communications gap integral to the battle of the sexes.

Difficult Conversations (Stone, Patton, Heen & Fisher)
Members of the Harvard Negotiation Project--which brought you the mega-bestseller Getting to YES--show you how to handle your most difficult conversations with confidence and skill.

Whether you're dealing with an underperforming employee, disagreeing with your spouse about money or child-rearing, negotiating with a difficult client, or simply saying "no," or "I'm sorry," or "I love you," we attempt or avoid difficult conversations every day.

Based on fifteen years of research at the Harvard Negotiation Project, Difficult Conversations walks you through a step-by-step proven approach to having your toughest conversations with less stress and more success. You will learn:

- how to start the conversation without defensiveness
- why what is not said is as important as what is
- ways of keeping and regaining your balance in the face of attacks and accusations
- how to decipher the underlying structure of every difficult conversation

Filled with examples from everyday life, Difficult Conversations will help you on the job, at home, or out in the world. It is a book you will turn to again and again for advice, practical skills, and reassurance.

Getting To Resolution:
Turning Conflict Into Collaboration (Stewart Levine)

What is the greatest impediment to productive and satisfying business and personal relationships? According to empowerment guru Stewart Levine, it's inadequate conflict resolution. Levine's seven- step model integrates two skills essential for success - collaboration and conflict resolution - and emphasizes the importance of a shift in attitude, assumptions, and approaches when facing a problem.

The Book Of Agreement: 10 Essential Elements For Getting The Results You Want (Stewart Levine)

For most people, negotiating an agreement feels adversarial. It is a process one tries to win. It is not viewed as a process that expresses a clear joint vision or a path to desired results. We have been conditioned to function in a "me vs. them" context.

Creating agreements for results, rather than negotiating agreements for protection, would provide much greater benefits. The conflicts most people get into are avoidable. Conflict develops because of differing expectations about what working with others will produce. Differences arise because these expectations have not been made explicit to everyone. People fail to make their expectations explicit because they never learned how.

The Book of Agreement provides a clear path through the minefields of conflict, to shared expectations.

The Eight Essential Steps to Conflict Resolution: Preserving Relationships at Work, at Home, and in the Community (Dudley Weeks)

This book teaches the reader a process towards better conflict management. It is not a hard process to learn; its not an easy process to use all the time, though. That being said, I recommend this book HIGHLY, especially to anyone who is looking for ways to make their home life, work life, or community life more enriching. -- a readers review

You're Never Upset for the Reason You Think!
(Layne & Paul Cutright)

If you are truly ready to enjoy relationships as "upset free zones" in which you experience deeper and more satisfying levels of love, connection, cooperation, creativity, synergy and more, then you will want to learn the secret revealed in this book. It will show you exactly how you can uncover the real cause of any problem or upset, stop the pain and halt the slide toward more upset and disappointment, every single time. The result: joyful, close and fulfilling relationships that are no longer poisoned by bad feelings, hurt, anger, and the inevitable "distance" that follows.

The book will introduce you to the newest and most powerful conflict resolution tool ever created - and the last you will ever need, called the Conscious Upset Resolution Exercise (CURE). The CURE is a simple, easy to learn, step-by-step method to neutralize, clarify, and resolve any upset you may encounter; with lovers, business partners, co-workers, family members, children and any other relationship that is important to you - even with unsettling news you see on the television or experiences you have in life. The CURE will show you how to:

- Cheat proof your romantic relationships.
- Stop those fights that never seem to end.
- Resolve the most difficult, seemingly impossible upsets.
- Reduce the duration of upsets from days, weeks, months or longer down to minutes or hours.
- Reduce the intensity of upsets and make them much less likely to occur again in the future
- Uncover what your emotions are really telling you.
- Re-ignite a fizzled out romance by removing the 3 hidden blocks to your partner's passion.
- Eliminate hurt feelings and anger in yourself and others.
- Expose "upset trigger points" and so you can avoid setting them off.
- Halt repetitive negative patterns of behavior and thinking that have led to continual heartache.

- Dissolve invisible blocks to your true happiness and well-being.
- Create an endless supply of confidence and personal power.
- Nurture life long relationships that only get better with time.
- Transform challenges into opportunities.
- Restore harmony and good feelings.
- Stop blaming yourself and others.
- Forgive yourself and others.
- Feel more in control of your life.
- Let go of things that no longer serve you.
- Overcome fear and feel safer.
- Gain a higher, more empowering perspective.
- Relieve emotional pain.

And much more . . .

Parent Effectiveness Training: The Proven Program For Raising Responsible Children (Thomas Gordon)

P.E.T., or Parent Effectiveness Training, began almost forty years ago as the first national parent-training program to teach parents how to communicate more effectively with kids and offer step-by-step advice to resolving family conflicts so everybody wins. This beloved classic is the most studied, highly praised, and proven parenting program in the world -- and it will work for you. Now revised for the first time since its initial publication, this groundbreaking guide will show you:

- How to avoid being a permissive parent
- How to listen so kids will talk to you and talk so kids will listen to you
- How to teach your children to "own" their problems and to solve them
- How to use the "No-Lose" method to resolve conflicts

Using the timeless methods of P.E.T. will have immediate results: less fighting, fewer tantrums and lies, no need for punishment.

Whether you have a toddler striking out for independence or a teenager who has already started rebelling, you'll find P.E.T. a compassionate, effective way to instill responsibility and create a nurturing family environment in which your child will thrive.

12 Hours to a Great Marriage:
A Step by Step Guide for Making Love Last
(Markman, Stanley, Jenkins & Blumberg)
For the past twenty-five years, the internationally renowned marital researchers from the Center for Marital and Family Studies at the University of Denver have been helping couples around the globe replace loneliness with connection, frustration with understanding, fear with confidence, instability with commitment, revenge with forgiveness, and monotony with passion.

Their program is called PREP®, short for the Prevention and Relationship Enhancement Program, and it's been so successful that its creators have been featured on Oprah, The Today Show, and 20/20, and its benefits have been documented in The New York Times, USA Today, Woman's Day, and Redbook.

Until now the only way you could experience this winning twelve-hour program was to attend a weekend workshop. But now, with 12 Hours to a Great Marriage, you can discover the simple, effective strategies that have helped thousands of couples - happily married, having issues, or planning to marry - to develop and protect their love, easily and at your own pace.

Each chapter covers one of the key ingredients of the program, like Being Best Friends, Having Fun Together, and Protecting and enhancing Your Love Life, and shows you how to take the steps that research shows are the basis for a long-term, healthy, loving marriage. By practicing the simple skills, taking the thought-provoking self-tests, doing the fun and innovative exercises, and reading real-life couples' inspiring and informative stories, you'll find that in twelve short hours you'll be well on your way to having that great marriage you've always dreamed of.

Communication Miracles For Couples (Doyle Barnett)

A lot of books about couples' communication give techniques that are too complicated, especially in the heat of the moment. Not so with the simple, powerfully effective methods in this little book. In just a few minutes, you'll learn how to help you and your partner feel totally loved, no matter how hurt or angry you are; never argue again; get your partner to really hear you and change; negotiate your way past any problem and repair broken trust; and find the best way to create lasting harmony and keep love alive. Whether you are a couple looking to enhance a good relationship or are deeply mired in problems, these techniques can produce miracles!

Conscious Loving:
The Journey Of Co-Commitment (Gay & Kathlyn Hendricks)

Here is a powerful new program that can clear away the unconscious agreements patterns that undermine even your best intentions. Through their own marriage and through twenty years' experience counseling more than one thousand couples, therapists Gay and Kathlyn Hendricks have developed precise strategies to help you create a vital partnership and enhance the energy, creativity, and happiness of each individual.

You will learn how to: Let go of power struggles and need for control; Balance needs for closeness and separateness; Increase intimacy by telling the "microscopic truth"; Communicate in a positive way that stops arguments; Make agreements you can keep; Allow more pleasure into your life. Addressed to individuals as well as to couples, Conscious Loving will heal old hurts and deepen your capacity for enjoyment, security, and enduing love.

Getting It Right the First Time: Creating a Healthy Marriage (Barry and Emily McCarthy)

Barry McCarthy, Ph.D., is a certified sex therapist and Professor of Psychology at American University. He has published extensively on couples and sexuality and given more than a hundred workshops around the world. Emily McCarthy, having worked for years as a speech therapist, now collaborates with her husband on books that address issues faced by married couples. Getting It Right the First Time provides the information every couple needs to know to understand what really makes a marriage work. Husband and wife team, Barry and Emily McCarthy share clear, helpful guidelines for creating a healthy marriage and reveal the strategies, skills, and attitudes that can help prevent disappointment, resentment, and alienation from entering the relationship.

How Can I Get Through To You?
Closing the Intimacy Gap Between Men and Women
(Terrence Real)
"What happened to the passion we started with? Why aren't we as close as we used to be?" Bestselling author and nationally renowned therapist Terrence Real unearths the causes of communication blocks between men and women in this groundbreaking work.

Relationships are in trouble; the demand for intimacy today must be met with new skills, and Real -- drawing on his pioneering work on male depression -- gives both men and women those skills, empowering women and connecting men, radically reversing the attitudes and emotional stumbling blocks of the patriarchal culture in which we were raised "Conventional therapy has failed most couples," Real writes, and with over 20 years of marriage and family counseling experience, he's qualified to judge.

Though traditional marital counseling has been prevalent for 30 years, divorce rates remain the same, and studies show that counseling has no lasting effect on either marital satisfaction or endurance. The author of I Don't Want to Talk About It, the national bestseller on male depression, Real is attuned to the characteristics of contemporary marriages and demonstrates insight into both male and female perspectives.

The fundamental problem, he argues, is American culture's deeply entrenched "psychological patriarchy," which devalues all things feminine (including healthy relationships) and wounds males at an early age by disconnecting them from themselves and others. Men can't relate, and women can't teach them how. Counseling, too, fails them both in a "collusion of silence" as to what's really wrong. Real's alternative is "relational recovery." Identifying a healthy marriage as one following the repeated pattern of "harmony, disharmony, and restoration," Real teaches five skills for accomplishing the crucial, ongoing task of repair: holding the relationship in high regard, preserving intimacy and relational (i.e., authentically connected) speaking, listening and negotiating.

With numerous scenes from his therapy sessions including quarrels most married couples will recognize, Real deftly shows readers how to transcend "our culture's anti-relational bias" and move "out of patriarchy into healthy relatedness."

How To Ruin A Perfectly Good Relationship (Love, Shulkin & Beaumon)
A laugh-inspiring book chockfull of the kind of "gotcha's" that contain serious lessons just beneath the surface. Pat Love and Sunny Shulkin hold up a big fun-house mirror to the kind of relationship behavior most of us are guilty of. Yup, there we are -- expecting but not giving ... paying attention to everyone but our partner... waiting for things to get better by themselves - so many relationship-busting behaviors, so little time!

Thing is, Pat and Sunny's observations may make us giggle, but they also reveal something very important: they show us what "growing apart" really looks like, day to day. And with most couples who split up giving this as the reason for the split, becoming conscious of how growing apart manifests a long the way seems one good way to prevent the ruination of a perfectly good relationship.

Lasting Love: The 5 Secrets of Growing a Vital, Conscious Relationship (Gay and Kathlyn Hendricks)
In this long-awaited follow-up to their book Conscious Loving, Kathlyn and Gay Hendricks take on two of the most pressing

problems that sap vitality and energy from our committed relationships: how to forge a closer relationship that still allows each partner full creative autonomy and how to generate the passion and preserve the harmony essential to keeping long-term partnerships alive and blooming.

Lasting Love grew out of the Hendricks' laboratory of their 23-year marriage as well as their 10-year study of more than 2,000 long-term, committed couples. They discovered that the most common couples conflicts could be traced to at least one of five root causes:

- An imbalance between the creative energy each partner contributes to the relationship
- A lack of emotional honesty
- An unwillingness to accept responsibility for everyday issues
- Deep-seated commitment problems
- A deficiency of daily appreciations

Using these insights as a starting point, the Hendricks devised a program based on five vital actions that simultaneously lead to a deeper flow of intimacy between partners and greater creative freedom for each individual:

- Spend time expressing your own creativity rather than focusing on "fixing" your partner
- Eliminate the barrier to speaking and hearing the truth about everything
- Break the cycle of blame and criticism
- Make commitments you can really stand by
- Become a master of verbal and nonverbal appreciation

Filled with helpful real-life scenarios and straightforward advice, Lasting Love is an essential guide for anyone involved in a long-term relationship who wants it not only to last but to flourish.

The Complete Idiot's Guide to The Perfect Marriage (Hilary Rich)

The Complete Idiot's Guide to the Perfect Marriage takes the anxiety out of working on your marriage. Feel confident discussing sex, money, even the in-laws! In this Complete Idiot's Guide you get down-to-earth strategies for improving your communication skills; idiot-proof steps for dealing with times of transition, such as moving and career changes; expert advice in an easy-to-understand format; and plenty of quizzes and exercises to help you along the way.

The Conscious Heart:
Seven Soul Choices That Create Your Relationship Destiny (Gay Hendricks & Kathlyn Hendricks)

The authors call it "practical magic"--the enchantment that occurs when couples act upon their highest intentions and deepest love.

Suddenly creativity and humor spill upon every page of life; intimacy is a given instead of a task; accountability and responsibility are freedoms rather than burdens. But getting to this magical state of being is the problem.

This book has all the right spells. Practical issues such as sex, aging, money, fights, and infidelity are all examined through the lens of a conscious heart. Without once faltering into surface solutions or cosmetic improvements, these world-renowned couples' therapists explore the seven choices that transform relationships from the inside out.

These seven simple--but powerful--choices enable couples to:

- Use conflict to create greater understanding
- Overcome the fears and defenses that block intimacy
- Resolve struggles for control
- Increase generosity and appreciation
- Deepen passion, commitment, and aliveness
- Release the creativity of each partner

Filled with numerous true-life stories--including how the authors survived and grew from their own midlife marital crisis--The Conscious Heart is an inspiring and instructive affirmation of the ultimate power of love.

The Truth About Love: The Highs, the Lows, and How You Can Make It Last Forever (Pat Love)
Love, a family and marriage therapist and coauthor of Hot Monogamy, here offers hope to those who feel that the flame of amour has gone out. She explains that all relationships go through predictable patterns and outlines the four up-and-down stages of love: Infatuation, Post-Rapture, Discovery, and Connection.

She explains how physiological changes account for some of the intense feelings brought on by initial attraction for example, how phenylethylamine, dopamine, and norpinephrine combine to create the natural high new lovers feel that helps them bond. Love goes on to explain that this heady infatuation stage, glorious as it may be, is not what love is really about. She explodes myths that can destroy relationships, such as "If my partner really loved me s/he'd know what I wanted all the time."

Other potential problems, as when a couple has different priorities for their relationship, are outlined and addressed. Including quizzes and lists of questions for discussion, this fluidly written book is recommended for all public libraries.

Have you ever believed that you have fallen out of love, or said "I still love him but I'm not IN LOVE anymore?" In this groundbreaking guide to the physiology and psychology of lasting love, Dr. Pat Love reveals that love has normal, predictable stages that include highs and lows, and that many couples mistake the lows for the end of love. The Truth About Love is an inspiring, practical guide that will teach you how not to break up before the breakthrough realization: You can create the true love you long for with the partner you already have.

Why Marriages Succeed or Fail: And How too Make Yours Last (John Gottman)

From psychology professor (Univ. of Washington) and marriage researcher Gottman: an upbeat, easy-to-follow manual based on research into the dynamics of married couples. Gottman describes his studies as being akin to a CAT scan of a living relationship and asserts that he's been able to predict the future of marriages with an accuracy rate of over 90 percent. In 1983 and 1986, his research team monitored more than a hundred married couples in Indiana and Illinois with electrodes, video cameras, and microphones as they attempted to work out real conflicts. Using the information derived from these sessions, Gottman concludes here that a lasting relationship results from a couple's ability to resolve conflicts through any of the three styles of problem-solving that are found in healthy marriages- - validating, conflict-avoiding, and volatile.

Numerous self-quizzes help couples determine the style that best suits them. Gottman points out, however, that couples whose interactions are marked by four characteristics--criticism, contempt, defensiveness, and withdrawal--are in trouble, and he includes self-tests for diagnosing these destructive tactics, as well as steps for countering them.

Interestingly, Gottman asserts that the basis of a stable marriage can be expressed mathematically: the ratio of positive to negative moments must be at least 5:1--and he offers a four-step program for breaking through negativity and allowing one's natural communication and problem-solving abilities to flourish. You can use his tested methods to evaluate, strengthen, and maintain your own long-term relationship.

You'll also learn:

- More sex doesn't necessarily improve a marriage
- Frequent arguing will not lead to divorce
- Financial problems do not always spell trouble in a relationship

- Wives who make sour facial expressions when their husbands talk are likely to be separated within four years
- There is a reason husbands withdraw from arguments -- and there's a way around it

If you love your mate but your relationship seem to be off track, then this book is for you.

Finding God Through Sex: Awakening The One Of Spirit Through The Two Of Flesh (David Deida and Ken Wilber)

Drawing on David Deida's own history of sexual spiritual practice, Finding God Through Sex presents a highly unconventional, liberating, demanding, blissful picture of what spiritual intimacy can be. intimacy,

Deida has designed and developed a remarkably effective program of transformative practices that fully addresses spiritual awakening in mind, body, and heart. He is a founding associate of Integral Institute and has taught and conducted research at the University of California Medical School in San Diego; University of California, Santa Cruz; San Jose State University; Lexington Institute, Boston; and Ecole Polytechnique in Paris, France.

Dancing With the Beloved: Opening Our Hearts to the Lessons of Love (Paul Ferrini)

I was moved to write a review on this most unusual and beautiful book. I found this book quite by accident. When I finished reading it, I thought it was the most important book I have ever read. For me, this book was about love, what love means, how we hold love in our hearts, and the depth of love in our souls. The book is interwoven with the most beautiful poetry. I found myself weeping at times, suddenly and unexpectedly. I believe I was weeping because the ideas expressed in this book were consistent with what I have always believed and held to be true, about the meaning of love, God, my spiritual path, and most especially, about my belief in soul-mates.

Falling In Love: Why We Choose the Lovers We Choose (Ayala Malach Pines)

Written by a renowned psychologist, this fascinating, engaging mix of research and clinical anecdotes discusses how we both consciously and unconsciously select those with whom we have intimate relationships and how we can, through successful relationships, help ourselves to grow as individuals.

Each chapter concludes with suggestions for those seeking love. It addresses every conceivable aspect of the psychology of mate selection in late 20th-century America, giving equal emphasis to social and clinical approaches to understanding romance. The book's first half is devoted to an ambitious and inclusive survey of the experimental literature on the general factors that influence attraction - for example, similarity, geographical proximity, physical beauty and social status.

The second half underscores the relevance of early childhood experiences with and between one's parents in understanding one's attraction to specific persons. Recent clinical theories suggest that we are attracted to persons who are in some critical way similar to our parents and who have the potential to directly stimulate, and thus heal, old childhood wounds. Pines also offers advice to those seeking love.

The Intelligent Heart: Transform Your Life with the Laws of Love   (David McArthur, Bruce McArthur)

Transform your life with the Laws of Love. Friends, lovers, parents, children, coworkers, and strangers will all be affected by your use of these simple yet powerful Laws of Love. A simple five-step process is all it takes to change your heart.

Scientific evidence from the electrophysiology lab at the Institute of HeartMath reveals that your ECG (heart rhythm) physically changes as you apply these simple laws. Happiness and health are within your reach each day, in any situation. Free yourself of those heart matters that age you. Whether a parent, spouse, or friend, you can be young-at-heart and happy in life.

**The Journey from Abandonment to Healing:
Turn the End of a Relationship into the Beginning of a New
Life (Susan Anderson)**
Like Dr. Elisabeth Kubler-Ross's groundbreaking On Death and
Dying, Susan Anderson's book clearly defines the five phases of a
different kind of grieving--grieving over a lost relationship. An
experienced professional who has specialized in helping people
with loss, heartbreak, and abandonment for more than two
decades, Susan Anderson gives this subject the serious attention
it deserves.

The Journey From Abandonment to Healing is designed to help
all victims of emotional breakups--whether they are suffering
from a recent loss, or a lingering wound from
the past; whether they are caught up in patterns that sabotage
their own relationships, or they're in a relationship where they
no longer feel loved. From the first stunning blow to starting
over, it provides a complete program for abandonment recovery.

The Divorce Recovery Journal (Linda C. Senn)
This is an interactive book full of insightful observations
splashed with humor and useful advice dealing with divorce and
starting over. Each page has space for personal journaling! Learn
how to ...

- Deal with your fears,
- Tame your anger,
- Address the restlessness, Cope with your soon-to-be-ex,
- Turn aloneness into a time of growth and renewal.

Finances

**Spiritual Economics: The Principles & Process of True
Prosperity (Eric Butterworth)**
"Spiritual Economics" is based on the spiritual laws and
dynamics of abundance. One of the key elements of this books
that raise it above a lot of spiritual law type writings is how
practical this book is. Eric Butterworth tackles some very
complex dynamics in a very pragmatic, understandable way. To

get maximum benefit out of this book, keep asking yourself this question, "How can I apply this to my life?" Integrate this material into your life and you will be amazed at how much more you can manifest. Some of the main ideas I got out of the book are: * I am responsible for all manifestations in my life, i.e. everything. * As I evolve, so does my manifestation potential evolve. * I need to do what I can with what I have where I am to manifest my desires. * I need to build the demand before the supply will manifest. I need to have the containers in which to put the supply once it comes. I need to become the kind of person who experiences that which I want before I can truly achieve it. * If things are tight, something has to give. I need to give selflessly of myself to the Universe.

Secrets of the Millionaire Mind:
Mastering The Inner Game Of Wealth (T Harv Ecker)

A witty pep talk for wealth-seekers is delivered by someone who's still amazed he's a millionaire. T. Harv Eker's book should shake even the most entrenched negative thinkers out of their easy chairs. Eker is bursting with energy and the need to teach you, and you, and yes, you, how to increase your wealth and quality of life by emulating his methods, which, oddly enough, are similar in many ways to methods taught for centuries about self-improvement.

The good news is this stuff is worth repeating as we tend to forget to maintain our momentum. Eker also imbues his lessons with easy-to-remember self-motivating techniques as you make your way to your abundant bliss.

Eker's claim to fame is that he took a $2,000 credit card loan, opened "one of the first fitness stores in North America," turned it into a chain of 10 within two and a half years and sold it in 1987 for a cool (but somewhat modest-seeming) $1.6 million. Now the Vancouver-based entrepreneur traverses the continent with his "Millionaire Mind Intensive Seminar," on which this debut motivational business manual is based.

What sets it apart is Eker's focus on the way people think and feel about money and his canny, class-based analyses of broad differences among groups. In rat-a-tat, "Let me explain" seminar-speak, Eker asks readers to think back to their childhoods and pick apart the lessons they passively absorbed from parents and others about money. With such psychological nuggets as "Rich people focus on opportunities / Poor people focus on obstacles,"

Eker puts a positive spin on stereotypes, arguing that poverty begins, or rather, is allowed to continue, in one's imagination first, with actual material life becoming a self-fulfilling prophecy. To that end, Eker counsels for admiration and against resentment, for positivity, self-promotion and thinking big and against wallowing, self-abnegation and small-mindedness.

While much of the advice is self-evident, Eker's contribution is permission to think of one's financial foibles as a kind of mental illness-one, he says, that has a ready set of cures.

The New Science of Getting Rich (Wallace Wattles)
Wattless book, first published in 1910, jumps into the present with the help of Eliza Fosss hip reading. Her voice sounds youthful yet educated, relaxed yet firmly engaged with the core of the lesson. The writing of this era is a delight--confident, erudite, precise.

The nonsectarian spiritual component will elevate listeners intentions and encourage their faith in the message. The author says that visualizing, thinking, and doing things in a certain way are the tools we need to create the abundant life we deserve.

He is especially lucid regarding the correct use of the will, which should be used not to control others, but to direct our own thoughts and actions toward the future of wealth we desire. T.W.
© AudioFile 2007, Portland, Maine-- Copyright © AudioFile, Portland, Maine --This text refers to the Audio CD edition.

Nine Steps To Financial Freedom: Practical & Spiritual Steps So You Can Stop Worrying   (Suze Orman)

Suze Orman has transformed the concept of personal finance for millions by teaching us how to gain control of our money -- so that money does not control us. She goes beyond the nuts and bolts of managing money to explore the psychological, even spiritual power money has in our lives.

The 9 Steps to Financial Freedom is the first personal finance book that gives you not only the knowledge of how to handle money, but also the will to break through all the barriers that hold you back. Combining real-life recommendations with the motivation to overcome financial anxieties, Orman offers the keys to providing for yourself and your family, including:

- seeing how your past holds the key to your financial future
- facing your fears and creating new truths
- trusting yourself more than you trust others
- being open to receiving all that you are meant to have
- understanding the lessons of the money cycle

As Orman shows, managing money is far more than a matter of balancing your checkbook or picking the right investments. It's about redefining financial freedom -- and realizing that you are worth far more than your money.

**Rich Dad, Poor Dad: What the Rich Teach Their Kids About Money That the Poor and Middle Class Do Not!
(Robert Kiyosaki)**

Personal-finance author and lecturer Robert Kiyosaki developed his unique economic perspective through exposure to a pair of disparate influences: his own highly educated but fiscally unstable father, and the multimillionaire eighth-grade dropout father of his closest friend. Rich Dad, Poor Dad lays out his the philosophy behind his relationship with money. His book compellingly advocates for the type of "financial literacy" that's never taught in schools.

Seven Stages Of Money Maturity: Understanding The Spirit & Value Of Money In Your Life (George Kinder)

Where do our attitudes about money come from--and how do they influence our lives? How can we approach financial issues with honesty and without fear? In this groundbreaking book, George Kinder, a Harvard-trained certified financial planner, demonstrates how we can literally transform our lives emotionally and financially by achieving "money maturity"--a full understanding of the spiritual and psychological issues surrounding our money lives. Kinder has created a revolutionary program that guides us through the Seven Stages of a revolutionary journey--one designed to help us uncover the roots of our attitudes about money, and attain true peace, freedom, and security in our financial lives. Learn how to:

- Understand feelings that impact taking financial action
- Develop understanding and knowledge about money
- Eliminate stress and anxiety around money
- Let go of old patterns and painful habits
- Approach money tasks with energy and optimism
- Design a money life that is fulfilling both financially and spiritually

The Abundance Book (John Randolph Price)

John Randolph Price writes about his own personal experiences to demonstrate that consciousness is the key to life, and that truly, nothing is impossible, including the manifestation of unlimited wealth and financial independence. This book is short, direct and to the point.

The Architecture Of All Abundance: Seven Foundations to Prosperity (Lenedra J. Carroll)

Lenedra Carroll, offers a memoir that speaks to her spiritual theories on creating abundance. The Architecture of All Abundance, her "rag to riches" life story, starts out when the author is a young girl growing up poor in a small Alaskan village and winds up with Carroll becoming a successful CEO of a global entertainment enterprise.

More than a memoir, this is more accurately an inspirational book on how you too can build a fulfilling life that includes plenty of spirit and prosperity. Carroll emphasizes the timeless truths of spiritual abundance--ones that readers have probably heard before: listen to your soul's voice, ask the right questions, make time for stillness, own the fear instead of avoiding it, remember that generosity generates prosperity.

Yet, like any effective teacher, Carroll has the ability to package these nuggets of wisdom with just the right anecdote or just the right phrasing so that it finally sinks in. It's not uncommon to find provocative passages such as, "We can all realize that while the fear is real, it is also true that what we fear is like a mirage rising off the heat of a projected or past pain." Although her structure of alternating poetry, personal stories, and spiritual advice makes the book slightly disjointed, Carroll's eloquence as a narrator ties it together.

The Energy Of Money, A spiritual guide to financial and personal fulfillment (Maria Nemeth)

The Energy of Money: A Spiritual Guide to Financial and Personal Fulfillment, outlines a distinctly unique approach to one of the most dominant yet forbidden topics in modern society: money, and how we deal with it. A clinical psychologist who once lost $35,000 in a fraudulent investment scheme, Nemeth learned from that ordeal how most of us develop relationships with money and the ways in which we subsequently can bring these in line with our actual dreams and realities.

She initially used this knowledge to start a workshop called You and Money, which eventually attracted more than 4,500 participants and led to the development of concepts now delineated in this book. Nemeth sets out "12 principles for personal fulfillment" designed to help readers "uncover the hidden landscape of beliefs, behavior patterns, and habits that underlie and sometimes subvert how you use money and other forms of energy."

The result is a refreshing, useful, and surprisingly accessible mixture of universal financial advice and the much rarer--but no less important--ethereal side of fiscal self-management. This powerhouse guide to prosperity presents twelve principles that will help you to:

- Uncover the hidden landscape of beliefs, patterns, and habits that underlie and sometimes subvert your everyday use of money and personal resources
- Tame the dragons of driven behavior and busyholism
- Defuse fears of deprivation and scarcity
- Embrace and work through paradox and confusion
- Consciously focus your money energy
- Clear yourself to receive the energy and support of others and the universe
- Develop and stay on your personal path to abundance

Through easy-to-follow exercises and meditations, effective worksheets, and other interactive processes, Dr. Nemeth will guide you to financial success and help you manifest your special contribution to the world.

The Soul Of Money: Transforming Your Relationship With Money & Life (Lynne Twist)
A wise and inspiring exploration of the connection between money and leading a fulfilling life. This compelling and fundamentally liberating book shows us that examining our attitudes toward money - earning it, spending it, and giving it away - can offer surprising insight into our lives, our values, and the essence of prosperity.

Lynne Twist is a global activist and fund-raiser who has raised more than $150 million in individual contributions for charitable causes. Through personal stories and practical advice, she demonstrates how we can replace feelings of scarcity, guilt, and burden with experiences of sufficiency, freedom, and purpose. She shares from her own life, a journey illuminated by remarkable encounters with the richest and poorest people on earth, from the famous (Mother Teresa and the Dalai Lama) to the anonymous but unforgettable heroes of everyday life.

Your Money Or Your Life (Joe Domingues & Vicki Robin)
More than three-quarters of a million people everywhere, from all walks of life, have found the keys to gaining control of their money--and their lives--in this comprehensive and revolutionary book on money management. This simple, nine-step program shows you how to:
- get out of debt and develop savings
- slow down the work-and-spend treadmill
- make values-based decisions about your spending
- save the planet while saving money

Wealth Without A Job: The Entrepreneur's Guide to Freedom and Security Beyond the Nine to Five Lifestyle (Phil Laut)
"People who earn lots of money from work they do not enjoy experience dissatisfaction because the money is never enough. Yet people who enjoy their work but earn so little that they are continually beset by financial problems sooner or later find that the problems overwhelm the enjoyment. Unless you are blessed with a trust fund to pay your bills, it's essential to devise a way for the work you love to provide an abundant income. This book provides you with that preparation." This book tells you what to do to construct a self-directed and financially successful career path, including how to:

- Determine your true purpose so that you choose a business that expresses your own values and calls forth your dormant passion
- Understand the fundamental changes in today's economic structure that virtually require self-actualizers to work for themselves
- Discover and adopt the characteristics that separate the wealthy from the others
- Earn the income you want from the work you love.

The Millionaire Course: A Visionary Plan For Creating The Life Of Your Dreams   (Marc Allen)
This book is an entire course, an easy in-depth guide to accomplishing one's dreams in life. Structured in results-minded lessons and interwoven with keys that offer sudden moments of understanding, the book helps the reader grasp new ways of thinking of, and attaining, wealth and fulfillment by doing what we love and adhering to compassionate values. Lesson topics include: "Imagine your ideal scene," "Discover your core beliefs, and learn how to change them," and "Grow at your own pace." Author Marc Allen offers both a life-changing philosophy and the specific tools - the business plan, the vocabulary, even resources for financing - needed to live the dream.

30 Lies about Money: Liberating Your Life, Liberating Your Money (Peter Koenig)
Much has been written about money-how to invest, save, become a millionaire, get out of debt, find financial freedom, change the monetary system, manage a business, hedge or save taxes. So what makes this book stand out from those already in the bookshops? Written for lay reader and expert alike, 30 Lies is a response to a newly emerging trend, where peoples' interest in money is not just to try and make more of it, but to understand better the causes of the increasingly contradictory money world they find themselves in.

Some of the issues: income inequity, increasing stress in making ends meet, decay of social systems, evaporation of pensions, polarisation of wealth, third-world indebtedness, Enrons and more. This book promises a simple understanding of these issues. But it goes further. This book not only exposes misleading flaws and "lies" in many universally accepted and unquestioned assumptions about money-it dissolves them!

Money Is Love: Reconnecting to the Sacred Origins Of Money (Barbara Wilder)
War, Poverty, hunger and crime are caused by the fear that surrounds money and its scarcity. Money is energy, and energy is limitless. Only our fear and our limited way of thinking make

money seem scarce. Using the tools and the exercises in this book, you can reconnect with the sacred origins of money, and direct the flow of money through your life and the world on a current of love, joy, goodwill and abundance.

Money is energy, and according to quantum physics the universe is made up of energy, which becomes matter only when information is focused on it. Wood is wood and not iron because of the information that forms the two different kinds of matter.

Too many of us labor under the belief that money is "a necessary evil," which is, more often than not, difficult to obtain. By changing our feelings about money from fear, anger, greed and scarcity, to love, joy, abundance and goodwill, we can change the way money moves through our lives and the lives of others all over the world.

"MONEY IS LOVE" teaches that as we begin to remove the negative thoughts and feelings that surround money and redefine money as love, we bring the power of love into all of our monetary transactions. This in turn opens our hearts to allow money to flow abundantly into our lives, creating a place of peace and joy. From this place of harmony we can then send money back out into the world on a flow of love and gratitude. Money healed can begin to heal all that it touches. And because money flows like blood through the planet, diseased it causes disease, but infused with love, money can become rejuvenating.

This work stands out from other transformational money theories, because it deals with not only healing our personal relationship with money, but with healing the money itself, returning it to its sacred roots and then using this money infused with love as an agent for healing "Money is the blood of the planet. Heal the money and we can heal the world.

Money is My Friend (Phil Laut)
Making money can be a fun, fascinating, creative enterprise. Phil Laut, whose financial seminars have helped thousands of men

and women from all walks of life dramatically increase their incomes, demonstrates how you can overcome the principle obstacles to making money such as guilt, fear, and feelings of helplessness or pressure.

Once you have made money your friend, you'll discover that increasing your income is a simple matter of using your imagination. Inside this unique book, you'll find exercises and self-tests to help you understand and utilize

- The four Laws of Wealth
- The six-step method for developing a purpose in life
- The simple seven-stage plan for finding the perfect career
- Twelve ideal techniques for creating a new self-image
- Fifteen priceless affirmations to change the way you think about money

And much more!

Money Magic: Unleashing Your True Potential For Prosperity & Fulfillment (Deborah L. Price)
Making, keeping, and enjoying money isn't just about investments, salaries, inheritances, or dividends, according to Deborah Price. It's also about the games people play around money and their character type in relation to it.

In Money Magic, Price shows readers how to stop making fear-based money choices and how to transform their relationship with money to obtain the wealth they desire.

The book is structured around eight "types": the Innocent (the ostrich approach); the Victim (blaming circumstances); the Warrior (conquering money); the Martyr (always rescuing someone); the Fool (gambler looking for a windfall); the Creator/Artist (regarding money as evil); the Tyrant (controlling through money); and the Magician (benefiting spiritually and financially from money). The Magician is the book's ideal, and Price offers exercises to help readers attain it.

Money Management For Those Who Don't Have Any (James L Paris)
Who says you need a big bank account and a pocketful of cash to enjoy the American Dream? Certainly not financial counselor Jim Paris. Jim shares how readers can handle their money in a God-honoring way and enjoy the benefits of sound financial planning. Based on biblical principles, Money Management for Those Who Don't Have Any contains more than 200 practical strategies, tips, and resources on how to-

- save money on credit cards
- buy a dream house-with nothing down
- build an investment account with little money

This handbook is the consummate guide to achieving financial success. Whether readers are broke or money is just tight, this book will help them attain their lifelong goals and dreams.

The Energy Of Money, A spiritual guide to financial and personal fulfillment (Maria Nemeth)
The Energy of Money: A Spiritual Guide to Financial and Personal Fulfillment, outlines a distinctly unique approach to one of the most dominant yet forbidden topics in modern society: money, and how we deal with it. A clinical psychologist who once lost $35,000 in a fraudulent investment scheme, Nemeth learned from that ordeal how most of us develop relationships with money and the ways in which we subsequently can bring these in line with our actual dreams and realities.

She initially used this knowledge to start a workshop called You and Money, which eventually attracted more than 4,500 participants and led to the development of concepts now delineated in this book. Nemeth sets out "12 principles for personal fulfillment" designed to help readers "uncover the hidden landscape of beliefs, behavior patterns, and habits that underlie and sometimes subvert how you use money and other forms of energy."

The result is a refreshing, useful, and surprisingly accessible mixture of universal financial advice and the much rarer--but no less important--ethereal side of fiscal self-management. This powerhouse guide to prosperity presents twelve principles that will help you to:

- Uncover the hidden landscape of beliefs, patterns, and habits that underlie and sometimes subvert your everyday use of money and personal resources
- Tame the dragons of driven behavior and 'busyholism'
- Defuse fears of deprivation and scarcity
- Embrace and work through paradox and confusion
- Consciously focus your money energy
- Clear yourself to receive the energy and support of others and the universe
- Develop and stay on your personal path to abundance

Through easy-to-follow exercises and meditations, effective worksheets, and other interactive processes, Dr. Nemeth will guide you to financial success and help you manifest your special contribution to the world.

Creating Money: Keys To Abundance (Sanaya Roman)
This book is a course in manifesting and creating abundance in your life, Section I, Creating Money, is a step-by-step guide to the art of manifesting. You will learn how to discover what you want, drawing things to you that will fulfill and satisfy you, that are even better than what you ask for. You will learn advanced techniques of manifesting and how to work with your own energy and the power of magnetism to draw things into your life in the fastest, easiest way possible. The second section of this book, Developing Mastery, will help you learn to work with and move through any blocks you may have about allowing abundance into your life. The third section, Creating Your Life's Work, will help you learn to make money and create abundance through doing the things you love.

You will learn many simple energy techniques to draw your ideal job to you, discover your life's work, and do what you love for a living. The fourth section, Having Money, is about having and increasing money and abundance in your life. You will learn how to create joy, peace, harmony, clarity, and self-love with your money, letting it flow and increase.

Health

Ageless Body, Timeless Mind (Deepak Chopra)
The message of his new book? "We are not victims of aging, sickness, and death. These are part of the scenery, not of the seer, who is immune to any form of change. This seer is the spirit, the expression of eternal being."

The basis for his belief, Chopra argues, is quantum physics and the work of such scientists as Heisenberg, Bohr and Einstein, with whose help Chopra tells us how to stave off the inevitable changes brought on by mortality and the passing of years. He advises us on how to defeat entropy, to believe enough to offer palpable resistance to processes of physical alteration, and to reinterpret your body such that renewal will come of it. He himself believes in a land where no one is old, and where we create our bodies as we create the experience of our world. He is also a proponent of the science of longevity, and cites research by doctors to back himself up when expounding upon it.

The Biology Of Belief: Unleashing The Power Of Consciousness, Matter And Miracles (Bruce H. Lipton)
The Biology of Belief is a groundbreaking work in the field of New Biology. Author Dr. Bruce Lipton is a former medical school professor and research scientist. His experiments, and those of other leading-edge scientists, have examined in great detail the processes by which cells receive information. The implications of this research radically change our understanding of life. It shows that genes and DNA do not control our biology; that instead DNA is controlled by signals from outside the cell, including the energetic messages emanating from our positive and negative thoughts.

Dr. Lipton's profoundly hopeful synthesis of the latest and best research in cell biology and quantum physics is being hailed as a major breakthrough showing that our bodies can be changed as we retrain our thinking.

Matrix Energetics: The Science & Art Of Transformation (Dr. Richard Bartlett)

In 1997, Dr. Richard Bartlett experienced an event that would redirect the entire course of his life. He suddenly discovered that by lightly touching his clients while at the same time applying focused intent, he could restore them to a physically, mentally, and spiritually balanced state, instantly shifting misalignments that had plagued them for years. Most astonishing of all, he could teach anyone how to do this. Now, for millions of people looking for empowerment in an age of declining and impersonal healthcare, Dr. Bartlett shares this phenomenon in a book full of explosive potential.

In Matrix Energetics, Dr. Bartlett builds upon his popular seminars to teach us how to access the discovery he has made -- a process that merges the science of subtle energy with our innate imaginations to produce measurable results. By applying forces known to modern physics, each of us can tap into states of healthy awareness from different moments -- in essence, travel in time -- and bring them into the present for immediate, profound results. As Dr. Bartlett clearly shows, this practice requires no special training, produces transformation in the blink of an eye, and is available to everyone who has a willingness to learn.

Matrix Energetics, The Science and Art of Transformation, provides an easily-reproducible, results-oriented process of change that draws on the fundamental principles embraced by the field of quantum physics.

This paradigm-busting book can teach anyone how to access their creative power to heal and transform their lives. Dr. Richard Bartlett discovered that what he once thought about the human body was just the tip of the iceberg -- after seeing change beneath his hands, and hearing about the invisible transformations that were often revealed later -- he knew that he had to pass along what he had discovered.

Perfect Health: The Complete Mind/Body Guide (Deepak Chopra)

This account of alternative healing comes from a seasoned, well-educated Western medical doctor. Chopra inspires us to discover the inner voices within ourselves to heal, transform and create a balanced state of all physical and psychological levels. The book describes how breakthroughs in physics and medicine were underscoring the validity of a 5,000-year-old medical system from ancient India known as Ayurveda ("the knowledge of life span" in Sanskrit).

Perfect Health goes on to describe how to apply the ancient wisdom of Ayurveda to everyday life. Although we experience our bodies as solid, they are in fact more like fires that are constantly being consumed and renewed. We grow new stomach linings every five days, for instance. Our skin is new every five weeks. Each year, fully 98 percent of the total number of atoms in our bodies is replaced.

Ayurveda gives us the tools to intervene at this quantum level, where we are being created anew each day. Ayurveda tells us that freedom from sickness depends on contacting our own awareness, bringing it into balance, and then extending that balance to the body.

Quantum Healing: Exploring The Frontiers Of Mind Body Medicine (Deepak Chopra)

Early on in Quantum Healing, Deepak Chopra asks an interesting question: Why, when your body mends a broken arm, is it not considered a miracle, but when your body rids itself of cancer, it is? Chopra believes the two phenomena spring from the same well, that the body is capable of doing much more than we assume it can.

He calls this ability to cure disease from within "quantum healing," and shows how we're all capable of it. He believes intelligence exists everywhere in our bodies, in each of our 50 trillion cells, and that therefore each cell knows how to heal itself. Here is an extraordinary new approach to healing by an extraordinary physician-writer -- a book filled with the mystery, wonder, and hope of people who have experienced seemingly miraculous recoveries from cancer and other serious illnesses.

Dr. Deepak Chopra, a respected New England endocrinologist, began his search for answers when he saw patients in his own practice who completely recovered after being given only a few months to live.

In the mid-1980's he returned to his native India to explore Aruyveda, humanities most ancient healing tradition. Now he has brought together the current research of Western medicine, neuroscience, and physics with the insights of Ayurvedic theory to show that the human body is controlled by a "network of intelligence" grounded in quantum reality.

Not a superficial psychological state, this intelligence lies deep enough to change the basic patterns that design our physiology -- with the potential to defeat cancer, heart disease, and even aging itself. in this inspiring and pioneering work, Dr. Chopra offers us both a fascinating intellectual journey and a deeply moving chronicle of hope and healing.

Spontaneous Healing: How To Discover & Embrace Your Body's Natural Ability To Maintain & Heal Itself (Andrew Weil, MD)
The body can heal itself. Spontaneous healing is not a miracle but a fact of biology--the result of the natural healing system that each one of us is born with. Drawing on case histories as well as medical techniques from around the world, Dr. Andrew Weil shows how spontaneous healing has worked to resolve life-threatening diseases, severe trauma, and chronic pain. Weil then outlines an eight-week program in which you'll discover:

- The truth about spontaneous healing and how it interacts with the mind
- The foods, vitamins, supplements, and tonic herbs that will help you enhance your innate healing powers
- Advice on how to avoid environmental toxins and reduce stress
- The strengths and weaknesses of conventional and alternative treatments
- Natural methods to ameliorate common kinds of illnesses

The Power Of The Mind To Heal (Joan Borysenko)

Joan Borysnko is a former cancer cell biologist with a degree from Harvard Medical School. She and her husband have written an informative and insightful book detailing the psychological and spiritual causes behind the diseases and ailments that afflict us. In easy-to-understand laymen's terms, the Borysenkos show the reader how our thoughts and actions affect our physical bodies and how we can thwart these fear-based afflictions.

The Power of the Mind to Heal will provide the readers with vital information to help themselves achieve long-lasting mental and physical health throughout all the years of their lives! The authors have integrated their considerable knowledge of medicine, metaphysics, spirituality, and alternative forms of healing into a beautiful book that reveals how we can use the amazing power of the mind to heal the physical and emotional ailments that afflict us.

Why People Don't Heal & How They Can (Caroline Myss)

For more than fifteen years, Caroline Myss has studied why some people heal, while others do not. In her previous book, Anatomy of the Spirit, Dr. Myss illuminated the hidden interactions of belief and body, soul and cell to show how, as she inimitably puts it, "your biography becomes your biology."

In this new book, she builds on her earlier teachings of the seven different energy centers of the body to provide a vital self-healing program for physical and spiritual disorders. With her characteristic no-nonsense style and high-voltage storytelling, she exposes and explodes the five myths about healing, explains the cultural and individual contexts in which people become physically and spiritually ill and invested in "woundology," and teaches new methods of working with the challenges that the seven energy centers embody.

You can Heal Your Life (Louise Hay)

Louise assists the reader in discovering and using their own creative power for healing. She explains how problems (disease) that exist in the body can be healed by knowing the mental/emotional cause and then applying a new pattern of thinking. The exercises and personal examples are very powerful.

Molecules Of Emotion: The Science Behind Mind-Body Medicine (Candace Pert)

Why do we feel the way we feel? How do our thoughts and emotions affect our health? Are our bodies and minds distinct from each other or do they function together as parts of an interconnected system?

In her groundbreaking book Molecules of Emotion, Candace Pert provides startling and decisive answers to these and other challenging questions that scientists and philosophers have pondered for centuries. Her pioneering research on how the chemicals inside our bodies form a dynamic information network, linking mind and body, is not only provocative, it is revolutionary.

By establishing the biomolecular basis for our emotions and explaining these new scientific developments in a clear and accessible way, Pert empowers us to understand ourselves, our feelings, and the connection between our minds and our bodies -- body-minds -- in ways we could never possibly have imagined before. Molecules of Emotion is a landmark work, full of insight and wisdom and possessing that rare power to change the way we see the world and ourselves.

Emotional Discipline:
The Power to Choose How You Feel (Charles C. Manz)
Emotions sometimes get the better of us all, but you can learn how to analyze and manage your emotional reactions in any situation. Emotional Discipline details five easy-to-learn steps and twenty five specific strategies for responding to your feelings in the present and preparing for emotional challenges in the future. This remarkable approach combines mind, body, and spirit to help you deal with arguably the most challenging part of the human condition: the constant fluctuations in how you feel that color your experience of life and limit your personal effectiveness. With Emotional Discipline you can gain the power to choose how you feel.

Emotional Intelligence (Daniel Goleman)
Everyone knows that high IQ is no guarantee of success, happiness, or virtue, but until Emotional Intelligence, we could only guess why. Daniel Goleman's brilliant report from the frontiers of psychology and neuroscience offers startling new insight into our "two minds"-the rational and the emotional-and how they together shape our destiny. Through vivid examples, Goleman delineates the five crucial skills of emotional intelligence, and shows how they determine our success in relationships, work, and even our physical well-being. What emerges is an entirely new way to talk about being smart.

Feelings Buried Alive Never Die (Karol Truman)
This book packs in an amazing amount of information in under 300 pages (some of these are lists of feelings and physical symptoms.) It is written very simply - no rocket science here. It addresses the origin of emotions and approaches emotions on the scientific, medical, and spiritual levels. This book appealed to both my wanting to know how my feelings came about and how to properly label them and my need for a simple tool or meditation to release the negative unresolved feelings which have keep me in my destructive patterns. I wish I had read this book when I was a teenager after an abusive upbringing, or while I was in college unmotivated to reach my full potential, or

before I made the decision to marry the wrong person. I am glad that I found it in time to work through some of the issues of my divorce and to continue on my quest for personal growth.

As the book explains the root to finding all of those answers is here - and shows you how to look inside yourself in a loving and compassionate way. It reiterates something we all know and easily forget - you are the truth you seek! (A readers review)

The HeartMath Solution: Engaging the Power of the Heart's Intelligence (Doc Lew Childre & Howard Martin)

The HeartMath Solution may easily be written off as a book too eccentric for widespread public consumption, and that's unfortunate. The title's a bit misleading--it's not about cardiac care and it's not about calculus, but rather how 30 years of research have shown that the heart's "intelligence" affects emotions and physical health--especially when it comes to handling stress--and specifically what you can do to balance heart rhythms, reduce stress hormones, and boost your immune system.

Yes, it sounds complicated, especially when you read that cardiologists worked with physicists and psychiatrists to develop the HeartMath program. But it's worth brushing off your skepticism and exploring the concepts in the Solution, as many employees of Fortune 500 companies have already done. The "intelligence" that the authors focus on refers to both the heart's "brain," or the 40,000 neurons found in the heart (the same number in the brain itself), and the intuitive signals the heart sends, including feelings of love, happiness, care, and appreciation. When such positive emotions are felt, they "not only change patterns of activity in the nervous system; they also reduce the production of the stress hormone cortisol." When there's less cortisol, there's more DHEA, the so-called fountain of youth hormone known to have anti-aging effects on many of the body's systems. The HeartMath Solution outlines 10 steps for harnessing the power of the heart's intelligence, including ways to manage your emotions and keep energy levels high. One of the most important is the "Freeze-Frame" technique for calming the nervous system, improving clarity of thought and perception, and boosting productivity (which is one of the many appealing features for those Fortune 500 companies).

Each step includes references to data proving its effectiveness, with handy summaries of the key points to remember at the end of each chapter. This is a book that takes a bit of scientific understanding and a lot of time to wade through, but one that could help you prevent stress from ruling your existence.

Web Resources
Many of these resources are designed to sell products such as books and CD lectures. However you can still find some very good material here. We will be expanding this list as other resources come to our attention so if you come across any websites you feel we should include, please share them.

Emotional Manifestation
http://www.christianpankhurst.com/manifesting/emotional-manifesting-part-1

How Intentions Manifest
www.stevepavlina.com/blog/2006/06/how-intentions-manifest/
A description of the process of manifesting your intentions. The Law of Attraction. simply says that you attract into your life whatever you think about. Your dominant thoughts will find a way to manifest. But the Law of Attraction gives rise to some tough questions that don't seem to have good answers. I would say, however, that these problems aren't caused by the Law of Attraction itself but rather by the Law of Attraction as applied to objective reality.

Intenders
www.intenders.com
The Intenders of the Highest Good show you how to have that which you desire come to you as easily and effortlessly as possible. We have rediscovered a simple method of self-

empowerment that we call The Intention Process which is making all of our dreams come true. We understand that our desires are in us to be fulfilled and that our thoughts create our world. We support and help one another to become as clear as possible in our words and our thoughts so that we can live our lives to the fullest.

Law of Attraction Discussion Group
http://groups.yahoo.com/group/Secret_Law_of_Attraction/join
You're invited to join our Yahoo group, the Secret Law of Attraction, where we'll be talking about: the Secret & Bleep movies, universal laws like the Law of Attraction, channeling Abraham-Hicks, your higher self and angels, the power of the mind and thought, ho'oponopono and the zero field, removing energy blockages with EFT, hypnotherapy, and Sedona, plus several exclusive articles by the greatest thinkers of today. This is a great way to connect with others interested in LOA.

Qualities that Attract/ Repel Abundance
www.orindaben.com/newsletter/attractabund.htm
A list of the 42 qualities that attract and repel money.

Zero Limits
http://www.zerolimits.info
This is the official website for the amazing new book by Dr. Joe Vitale and Dr. Ihaleakala Hew Len, titled "Zero Limits." It explains the true story of the unusual therapist who helped heal an entire ward of mentally ill criminals -- without seeing any of them. The book reveals his method. It reveals the true cause for everything that happens to you, and how to "clean" the negativity so you can re-connect with the Divine.

The Law of Attraction
www.TheMastersOfTheSecret.com
This FREE online course, called The Masters of The Secret with Bill Harris, reveals the most powerful concepts and practical information about how to implement The Secret in your life - and how to get all the benefits, right now.

Secret Law of Attraction
www.borntomanifest.com
We are on the cutting edge of an incredible time in human history - a great awakening. We stand at a pivotal moment in time where mankind stands to expand its consciousness and transcend the holographic illusion of what is considered reality. The Law of Attraction, the Art of Conscious Creation, the Secret, the Bible's "what you sow you reap" - whatever tradition we wish to call it - the great avatars and masters throughout history have always taught...

Universal Laws
http://www.universallawstoday.com
What are these Universal Laws ? You can think of these laws as "spiritual laws" or "energy laws" because everything in the universe is comprised of energy. These laws are in affect whether you are aware of them or not. Just like the law of gravity -- you may not understand it but that does not change the effect it can have if you jump off of a building, you WILL still hit the ground. The same holds true for these Laws of the Universe and once you understand them you can have more control over what it is that you are experiencing in your life each and every day. You can use these laws to change your life.

United World Healing
http://www.unitedworldhealing.org
Our mission is to harness the conscious intent of people and organizations to synergistically create a healthy, compassionate world. We are uniting people to visualize and manifest a better world--one that protects, respects and reveres mankind, animal kind and the environment.

"O" Dream Board: Envision Your Best Life
http://www.oprah.com/spirit/O-Dream-Board-Envision-Your-Best-Life
People have created vision boards for years using images from magazines on corkboards or poster boards but they weren't very portable. Since many of us spend our days on the computer, O

Dream Board can be right there with you on your desktop to serve as a daily reminder of your aspirations and what you want your life to be. What do you want in your life? What images represent your dreams? What words inspire you to move forward? Capture them with O Dream Board. Get clear about your goals, your hopes and your vision for your life. Make the connection to turn your dreams into reality every day. O Dream Board is a free desktop application available to all Oprah.com members that you'll need to download. It's easy and quick!

PostScript

Needless to say, I have read a ton of books on the subject of conscious creation, manifestation and the law of attraction. Some were excellent and some just mediocre. In 2015, after much of this was already written, I came a new author who burst on to the scene with a phenomenal twenty three books in just two years.

I like to refer to Richard Dotts as a 'manifestation heretic' and I mean this as a high compliment. Unlike most books on the subject, including the one you just read, he approaches the whole subject of conscious creation as basically a spiritual endeavor. Bottom line; when you get the interior right, then the exterior takes care of itself.

OK, maybe that is a slight simplification but it really is the essence of his books as I understand them. It's ultimately about the inner work and the inner world of consciousness. When this is right, everything falls in to place. As much as I am given to goals, intentions, visualizations and all of the various techniques which have worked for me, I will have to agree with Dotts that in the long run, it comes down to who you are and not what you do. As the saying goes, your world is first and foremost a reflection of who you are and not just what you do. So his basic teaching is 'work on the who, and not the do.' Below is a list of his books as of this printing. They are all different and yet similar. They are also very readable and can be found on amazon.com. I highly recommend these.

- What To Do When You Are Stuck
- Banned Money Secrets
- Allowing Divine Intervention
- It Is Done: The Final Step To Instant Manifestations
- Banned Manifestation Secrets of Ancient Spiritual Masters
- Playing In Time & Space
- The Magic Feeling Which Creates Instant Manifestations
- Dollars Flow To Me Easily
- Come Sit With Me: How To Desire Nothing and Manifest Everything
- Come Sit With Me
- Mastering The Manifestation Paradox
- Today I Am Free: Manifesting Through Deep Inner Changes
- Light Touch Manifestation: How To Shape The Energy Field To Attract You Want
- Infinite Manifestations: The Power Of Stopping At Nothing
- Afternoon Manifestations
- Inner Confirmation For Outer Manifestation
- The 95-5 Code For Activating The Law Of Attraction
- Spontaneous Manifestation From Zero: Tapping Into The Universal Flow
- Thoughtless Magic & Manifestations
- Your Greatest Gift: That Unlocks All Manifestation
- Manifestation Pathways: Letting Your Good Be There
- The Magic Path of Intuition

Made in the USA
Lexington, KY
25 May 2016